Against Cheap Grace in a World Come of Age

Martin Luther King, Jr. Memorial Studies in Religion, Culture, and Social Development

Mozella G. Mitchell
General Editor

Vol. 9

PETER LANG
New York • Washington, D.C./Baltimore • Bern
Frankfurt am Main • Berlin • Brussels • Vienna • Oxford

Ralph Garlin Clingan

Against Cheap Grace in a World Come of Age

An Intellectual Biography of Clayton Powell, 1865–1953

PETER LANG
New York • Washington, D.C./Baltimore • Bern
Frankfurt am Main • Berlin • Brussels • Vienna • Oxford

Library of Congress Cataloging-in-Publication Data

Clingan, Ralph Garlin.
Against cheap grace in a world come of age: an intellectual biography
of Clayton Powell, 1865–1953 / Ralph Garlin Clingan.
p. cm. — (Martin Luther King, Jr. memorial studies in religion,
culture, and social development; vol. 9)
Includes bibliographical references and index.
1. Powell, A. Clayton (Adam Clayton), 1865–1953. I. Series.
BX6455.P63 C57   286'.1'092—dc21   2001038894
ISBN 0-8204-5770-1
ISSN 1052-181X

Die Deutsche Bibliothek-CIP-Einheitsaufnahme

Clingan, Ralph Garlin:
Against cheap grace in a world come of age: an intellectual biography
of Clayton Powell, 1865–1953 / Ralph Garlin Clingan.
–New York; Washington, D.C./Baltimore; Bern;
Frankfurt am Main; Berlin; Brussels; Vienna; Oxford: Lang.
(Martin Luther King, Jr. memorial studies in religion,
culture, and social development; Vol. 9)
ISBN 0-8204-5770-1

The cover photograph of Rev. Clayton Powell is from
The New Haven Register and used by permission of The Connecticut
Afro-American Society, The Ethnic Heritage Center, Southern
Connecticut State University, New Haven, CT

The paper in this book meets the guidelines for permanence and durability
of the Committee on Production Guidelines for Book Longevity
of the Council of Library Resources.

© 2002 Peter Lang Publishing, Inc., New York

All rights reserved.
Reprint or reproduction, even partially, in all forms such as microfilm,
xerography, microfiche, microcard, and offset strictly prohibited.

Printed in the United States of America

Dedicated with love and gratitude to

Maria Margaret Ambrose Clingan

Table of Contents

Introduction		ix
A Powell Chronology		xv
Chapter One	A Prophet of Liberation	1
Chapter Two	Spiritual Biblical Hermeneutics	17
Chapter Three	Ethical Progress Through Emotion	35
Chapter Four	Progress Through the Love of Jesus	49
Chapter Five	Toward a Progressive Church	63
Chapter Six	Powell's Hermeneutics and Beyond	75
Bibliography		95
Scripture Index		113
Names Index		117

Introduction

"Cheap grace" and "world come of age" are only two phrases Clayton Powell coins during his long life, 1865–1953, that Dietrich Bonhoeffer (1906–45) uses in his post–Harlem works. He thinks Fundamentalism a better theology than either Liberal or Social Gospel options until he spends time with Powell. Then, the Social Gospel leaves an impression on him for a long time to come (Renate Wind, *A Spoke in the Wheel: The Life of Dietrich Bonhoeffer,* 33f). Powell's Biblical hermeneutics is a distinctive development in the history of Biblical interpretation in North America. Comparing his hermeneutics with those of the sources he claims, I disclose his hermeneutics. He influences others, including, as Ruth Zerner notes, a German Sunday School Teacher, Bonhoeffer (Zerner, "Dietrich Bonhoeffer's American Experiences: People, Letters and Papers from Union Seminary," *Union Seminary Quarterly Review*, Summer, 1976, 266–72). After learning from Powell, he calls others to work against cheap grace in a world come of age because they love Jesus, phrases he hears Powell use in spite of death threats from Fundamentalists during the six months he attends Abyssinian Baptist Church with Union Seminary classmate Frank Fisher. Marion and Paul Lehmann show him African America originally and Reinhold Niebuhr requires classes to read African–American authors. One of them, Countee Cullen, impresses him so much that he mentions him in his letters (Wind, 34f and Bonhoeffer, *No Rusty Swords*, 112). My work shows similarities and differences between Powell and the sources William Ferris notes him reading, revealing a distinctive, progressive Biblical hermeneutics. I correct mistaken impressions of Powell and bring his views into dialogue with scholars interested in Bonhoeffer's experience of six months, 1930–31, which changes him from mere theo–logian to real Christian, in his own words. He experiences a seriously well thought out program of personal and social moral progress designed to emotionalize the love of Jesus Christ in him, the central focal point of Powell's ministry.

Powell is not a Fundamentalist interpreter of the Bible, contrary to what other authors think. He is a prophetic, Spiritual interpreter of the Bible, using Frederick Douglass' works and the Spirituals' interpretation of the Bible and the theology of Samuel Harris of Yale Divinity School. Far from rejecting education or intellectual study, he worships education and includes scholarly preparation in his Spirituality. He is a manuscript preacher with dramatic delivery skills who moves people emotionally and intellectually to ethical action. A parishioner notes that unlike the rhetoricians of advertising, he speaks not to sell or promote the Gospel but to move people to do the Gospel. Nor is he an individualist, rather he allows the Spirit of the Bible to interpret him, his community and the world as an inter-related whole.

Not self-centered, Powell centers himself and his ministry on Jesus Christ as Savior and Lord. A self-confessed hoodlum, his conversion occurs during the Spirit-induced coma a Rev. Houston experiences. In his ministry, he keeps his hands full of the Bible, baptismal candidates, bread, wine, marriages, funerals, revivals, preaching engagements, ecumenical, economic, education and political labors. He stays in ministry despite the poverty of his first Call in Philadelphia, his beginning in New Haven and the cold-water flat in a whore-house hotel near Manhattan's theater district at the start of his Abyssinian ministry, not to mention thousands of death threats that come through the postal service and appear in newspapers. Daily he chooses to swim against the tides of racism, Fundamentalism and Liberalism to keep Christ Jesus the center of his life and ministry. The Sermon on the Mount, Matthew 5-7, is his curriculum and the church in Jerusalem his model for a new reformation of the Church.

Powell advocates the equal status and power of women in marriage, church, society, culture and religion; progressive for his time. The crowning achievement of his career is hiring M. Virginia Wood to be the first ever woman Youth Minister in any Church. He educates and pays a number of women for missionary service in Africa and for mission on the home front. Income from the sale of sermon copies finances his discreet funding of higher educations for Harlem women as well as men while publicly working with John Dewey at Columbia, to make Abyssinian an extension campus for Columbia's nursing and Education schools, open to women and men from the community. He builds a community center in Harlem based on the dream of Nannie

Helen Burroughs of the District of Columbia, an equal partner in mission and ministry.

The mission of African people, whose destiny God intertwines with that of Europeans in the U. S., is to deepen the emotions of sympathy and love through a church that freely and joyfully hears and obeys Jesus, liberating oppressive and oppressed peoples and churches to achieve justice, mercy and peace. Powell often says people who love are superior to people who hate. That is why he holds Mohandas Gandhi, a Progressive Hindu, as the greatest embodiment of moral force in the world. Paul Lehmann worries that Bonhoeffer spends too much time in Harlem. Bonhoeffer replies, not enough. If he spends more time in Harlem, maybe he would share Powell's egalitarian view of women, Jews and Hindus. Is his admiration of Gandhi the stimulus for Bonhoeffer's desire to go to India; his use of the Sermon on the Mount and the phrases cheap grace and world come of age so important to the young German Sunday School Teacher that he uses them freely?

My first motive for undertaking the project is the opinion of members and elders of the church I served between 1970 and 1974 that I sound like the senior Powell, under whose preaching they were converted. How could that be? Reading Eberhard Bethge's biography of Bonhoeffer, I found that he was at Abyssinian, 1930–31. Could Powell have influenced him so much that, through my study of him, Powell influenced me, too? The question proved too intriguing to resist. Finally, from 1987 to 1997, it consumed me until I wrote this book.

Clayton Powell is a distinctively radical, independent mind at work during a time of vast social and global change. I demonstrate his freedom of thought by bringing his works into dialogue with important authorities in his self–chosen context as noted by Ferris, who befriended him in New Haven and visited him frequently during his New York career. I discovered much material pertinent to today's philosophical–hermeneutical, psychological ethics and theological debates. My conclusion establishes a new hermeneutics and homiletics.

Moreover, Powell's formative influence on the young Dietrich Bonhoeffer's post–Harlem works is traced in this book. Therewith, Powell converses with Bonhoeffer scholars trying to discern influences that altered his theological direction during 1930–31, when, as a visiting scholar at Union Theological Seminary in New York City, he eschewed two Lutheran congregations (St. Peter's, Bronx and Trinity, Manhattan) and chose Abyssinian Baptist Church in Harlem with fellow student Fisher, who, with other Bachelor of Divinity (now Master of Divinity) students, Union required to go there. Bonhoeffer went, not be-

Cause he had to (he was a Sloan Fellow), but because he heard the preaching of the Gospel of Jesus Christ the Savior of sinners there and not at Fundamentalist Broadway Presbyterian, St. Peter's or Trinity Lutheran or Liberal Riverside Church. My findings cast doubt on all Fundamentalist appropriation of and caricatures of Powell. Thoroughly examining the preacher of the Gospel who drew him, surprises popped up along the way which may delight and inform others as much as me.

Through Ferris's remarks in Powell's autobiography I learn about very surprising figures in European, North American and world history about whom I neither hear nor read anything as part of my schooling up to that point. Harris of Yale, their first academic theologian and the last of the rose–bespectacled Federal Theologians; Benjamin Kidd, the English Darwinian who repented of his views after World War One. His posthumous *Science of Power* influences so many, not only Powell. Giovanni Papini, a former Italian anarchist who writes a biographical novel of Jesus that Powell reads. Just as surprising is William James Durant, story–teller of Western Philosophers. Unaware of these men, their works and their individual importance to the study of early 20th century American and world history, other scholars are mis–taken about Powell and, subsequently, Bonhoeffer.

Each chapter follows roughly the same routine. I develop the work of each influential person in his critical and historical context, just as I exegete a text of Scripture. Then, I weave in parts of Powell's work, both the parts that show the influence of the figure he reads and parts that show his own distinctive ways. Expository writing can be boring, so I vary the form, as much to keep myself from nodding off as to interest you.

My thanks to Scott Holland for his September, 2000 article in *Cross Currents Magazine*, "Dietrich Bonhoeffer's New York: First We Take Manhattan, Then on to Berlin," in which he relies on my doctoral dissertation of 1997 at Drew University. Thanks to Ruth Zerner for her 1976 lecture and *Union Seminary Quarterly Review* article on Bonhoeffer at Union Seminary and Abyssinian Church from his and his friends' books, letters and interviews, in which she appreciates the emotionalization Bonhoeffer enjoys at Abyssinian (Zerner, 263, 266–70, 81). She does not include Powell's deliberate, well–thought–out program and style of ministry as a scholarly manuscript preacher. Thanks to Renate Wind and her *Dietrich Bonhoeffer: A Spoke in the Wheel*, 1990. She explores Abyssinian Church but does not comprehend the intellectual depth of Powell's program of ethical progress, especially in race relations, through the emotionalization of Jesus Christ's ideal of universal love using the works of Harris and Kidd. Thanks go to Josiah Young for *No Difference in the Fare: Dietrich Bonhoeffer and the Problem of Racism*, 1998, in which he explores more about Powell than the others through his autobiography, overlooking references to Ferris and Rienzi Lemus' evaluation of his appropriation of Kidd's program based on Auguste Comte's emotionalization of the ideal which both wrote, if women lead, enables Western Civilization to make moral progress. Most sincere thanks to Mozella Mitchell of The University of South Florida, editor of the series, *Martin Luther King, Jr. Memorial Studies in Religion, Culture and Social Development* for her generous praise of my work. Thanks also to Phyllis Korper, Acquisitions Editor at Peter Lang, AG for generously accepting my effort; and the marketing department of Peter Lang AG. Thanks to many people who helped me along the way at Immanuel Church, New Haven, Abyssinian Church (especially Rev. Tino "like Boom" Woodard and Rev. Calvin Butts, D. Min.), New York, The American Baptist Convention Headquarters, Mount Vernon, Pennsylvania, Lincoln University, Pennsylvania, The Schomburg Branch of the New York City Public Library in Harlem and The Library of Atlanta University, on the Board of which I served from 1980 to 1988 when I taught there. Production Supervisor Jacqueline Pavlovic nurtured me through learning how to be my own editor and producer. She took time to have her second baby and returned to carry me the rest of the way. Thanks.

Thanks go to Melva Costen, other faculty colleagues and students in The Interdenominational Theological Center for encouraging me to explore this road not taken. This work differs substantially from my dissertation. The dissertation displays Powell as an intellectually able, complex figure, against the tide of scholarly treatments that caricature him as the opposite of what he is, a Fundamentalist. This book displays the obvious contours of his influence on Dietrich Bonhoeffer and implies that, through *The Cost of Discipleship*, the Powell–influenced Bonhoeffer work was included by Karl Barth in his *Church Dogmatics*. As such, this is a work of intellectual biography in African–American studies and ecumenically, the work of a Presbyterian showing the influence of a Baptist on a Lutheran. Much fun for me and, I hope, for you, too.

Have a good read and thanks for your interest.

Ralph Garlin Clingan
Bloomfield, New Jersey

A Powell Chronology

1865 Born May 5 near Franklin's Mill near convergence of Maggotty and Soak Creeks in Franklin County, Virginia, to African–Choctaw–German mother, Sally Dunning, unknown father, probably her former owner, a German, killed in battle.

1871 Starts school, teacher Jake Bowles cites his brilliance.

1872 Ex–slave stepfather, Anthony Powell, gives him a copy of John's Gospel, saying he will send Clayton to school when he can read it, which he does, then and there; thereafter a voracious reader; disillusionment with Fundamentalists.

1875 Family moves to Tompkin's Farm near Colesburg, West Virginia. Meets Mattie Schaeffer at school where Addie Bowles knows not enough Math to take him beyond simple fractions. Leaves school in 1878 at 13 years of age.

1884 Moves to Rendville, Ohio, away from family, works in Rend's coal mine and emulates the hoodlum style of the lead character in pulp fiction series, *Peck's Bad Boy*.

1885 Goes into a church one evening during a revival preached by D. B. Houston, the pastor, who experiences a Spiritual coma which converts Powell, who becomes Sunday School Secretary, reads the Bible and other books, serves as Deputy Marshall under Mayor Tuppins, works at Rendville Academy as Janitor while a student, reads Frederick Douglass, Blanche Bruce, John Langston, John Lynch, Senator Revills and Governor Pinchback for the first time.

1887 Moves to the District of Columbia, works at Howard House, reads books 2–3 hours daily, all of Shakespeare and the Bible.

1888 A desire to preach seizes him so he enters Wayland College and Seminary, founder George Merrill Prentiss King from Maine influences him, and where Mattie Schaeffer studies.

1890 Marries Mattie Fletcher Schaeffer.

1892 Completes both the college and seminary curricula at Way-Land, delivers Class Oration, "The Elevation of the Masses–the Hope of the Race," receives ordination to ministry, accepts Call to a Minneapolis church, which wants the former Pastor back, so he returns East to find that while he is away, his mother Sally dies. Serves Ebenezer Baptist Church, Philadelphia; he and Mattie work as domestics at Atlantic City, New Jersey, hotels during summer to make ends meet.

1893 Accepts Call to Immanuel Baptist Church, New Haven, Connecticut, delivers lectures throughout New England, "The Stumbling Blocks of the Race," and "My Two Black Cats."

1895–96 Studies as special student at Yale Divinity School, where students including William Ferris attend Immanuel and help shape his future career. Writes and publishes *A Souvenir of Immanuel Baptist Church–Its Pastors and Members*, at a low ebb financially, truly dedicates life to ministry. Attends Atlanta Exposition, hears fellow Franklin County Virginian Booker Washington, hailed by President Cleveland, first ex–slave to address predominantly European audience, delivers speech, "The Five Handcuffs of My Race," after which Powell adds his version, "Broken, But Not Off." Buys a house in New Haven with income from "My Two Black Cats." Studies under Samuel Harris, delivers lectures to standing room only crowds in San Diego, Los Angeles and San Francisco, favorable editorial about him in *California Eagle*. Works with Isaac Napoleon Porter and others to wield power in New Haven politics.

1898 Blanche Powell is born in New Haven.

1900 Delegate to Christian Endeavor Convention in London, UK, travels in France, subsequent lecture, "Twelve Days in Balmy France," sells more than all other lectures. Further study of the Abolitionists produces three more lectures, "John Brown," "William Lloyd Garrison," and "The Religion of Frederick Douglass."

1902 *The Colored American Magazine* publishes "The Religion of Frederick Douglass."

1904 Wayland, merged with other African schools to form Virginia University, bestows Doctor of Divinity on Powell.

1906 Preaches interdenominational unity to achieve global evangelism in "The Significance of the Hour" at dedication of First African Baptist Church, Philadelphia, delivers paper on William L. Garrison at last meeting of New Haven clergy, among whom he organizes inter-racial, interdenominational pulpit exchanges and city-wide revivals. After attending DuBois' Niagara Conference, brings him to deliver orations and organize chapters of the NAACP. Bonhoeffer is born.

1908 After increasing Immanuel's membership more than two-thirds, paying off all debts, freeing church from European-American rule, changing the time of worship from afternoon to morning, accepts Call to Abyssinian Baptist Church in New York, and is feted three times before leaving New Haven. Abyssinian has 1600 members, is in a Red-light district and owes large debts. Cold-water apartment his family shares is in a Hotel populated by prostitutes. Adam, Jr. is born.

1909 Cleans prostitution out of neighborhood. Sermon, "Little Foxes," against prostitution, *New York Age* publishes. Leads a month-long revival in Indianapolis, *Christian Banner* and *The Indianapolis Star* publish "An Awful Whirlwind," a sermon about sin and grace. Preaches first of seven ecumenical revivals for YMCA, Baltimore, reports *The Afro-American*. Two sermons on race relations, "Watch Your Step" and "Some Don'ts to Be Remembered," published in *Age*. Serves on Boards of NAACP and Urban League.

1911 "A Model Church," from Acts 5.4, is written and becomes his most–often delivered sermon, part of his campaign to move Abyssinian to Harlem from 40th street in Manhattan. *Age* Publishes "A Graceless Church," an assault against cheap grace.

1912 *Age* publishes two more sermons.

1913 More of his work appears in *Age*.

1914 *Age* publishes another assault on cheap grace, "American Religion an Abomination with God." Marcus Garvey trans– forms Harlem, Powell, inspires new wave of radical social action by Urban League and NAACP. Urban League starts magazine, *Opportunity,* with his "The Church in Social Work" as lead article.

1915 Criticizes African–Americans for not patronizing African– American business and professional people. Denied political power, at least Africans can save money, engage in business and buy property (Seth Scheimer, *Negro Mecca: A History of the Negro in New York City, 1865–1920,* 70).

1918 Publishes first book, in the wake of the First World War, *Patriotism and the Negro.* Asks state of New York National Baptist Convention to help fund building of Community Center to fulfill the vision of Nannie Helen Burroughs. Re– jected 92–8, he comes back, builds the Center anyway, never asks for anything from anyone again. Delivers "The Valley of Dry Bones" for the first time.

1921 Threatens to resign if church will not move to Harlem; resignation rejected, plans made to build a new church.

1922 Builds church in Harlem, calls Rev. Horatio Hill from Yale to di– rect Community House, organizes Highways and Hedges Society to care for every abandoned child in Harlem, sends and salaries Laura Bayne, Abyssinian Nursing School graduate as missionary to Congo (Zaire) Africa, three more women follow. School of Re– ligious Education includes extension campuses of Columbia's Nursing and Education departments, has four boys' and six girls' clubs, Thursday Community forums, Sunday Evening Community Lyceums, a Book-a-Month Club, raises money for every Church building in Harlem, builds a Medical Center, now Harlem Hospital, and National Training School for Women and Girls run by Nannie Helen Burroughs in The District of Columbia, Tuskegee-Hampton Institute, Fisk and Virginia Union Universities. Abyssinian endows the first Professorial chair established by African-Americans, at Virginia Union.

1924 Exhaustion from working three years without a break gets to him, so Powell accepts a 103-day tour of Europe, Palestine and Egypt from Abyssinian, develops lectures on each town affected by Jesus and four lectures on his travels. Howard University confers a D. D. on him.

1925 Union Seminary, New York, invites Powell to preach in chapel for the first time. Union requires B. D. students to visit Abyssinian. Lectures about his Africa trip on West Coast.

1926 Blanche dies because of misdiagnosis. Powell builds first African-American home for the elderly.

1927 *Negro Pulpit Opinion* publishes "The Bible More Than Literature."

1928 Harmon Foundation honors Powell for notable achievement in religious education. Abyssinian mortgage burning. *New York World*, *Negro Pulpit Opinion* and *The Pittsburgh Courier* publish Powell's "Progress-the Law of Life."

1929 Twentieth anniversary celebration at Abyssinian. Lectures at Virginia Seminary and College, Virginian Union, North Carolina College for Negroes, West Virginian State College, Fisk, Howard and Shaw Universities, National Training School for Women and Girls, City College of New York and First of three annual lectures on race relations at Colgate, Where his son, Adam matriculates, "Mob Rule-Its Causes and Cure," "Race Relations," and "Rules of the Road." Preaches the most controversial sermon of his career, the one that provokes the most death threats, "Lifting Up a Standard for the

People," published in *New York Age.*" Death threats include one from African–American Fundamentalists calling themselves The Black Hand, which appears in Baltimore's *The Afro–American* December 21, 1929 and from an Arkansas European–American named Vandlandingham.

1930 Powell suffers nervous breakdown from overwork, sick three months. Rev. Hill leaves and Adam graduates from Colgate, becomes Business Manager at Abyssinian and preaches his father's sermon until he returns to work in December. He meets the Great Depression with Free Food Kitchen, Unemployment Relief Fund and Relief Bureau. Repeats "A Model Church," and new sermons, "A Naked God," and "A Hungry God," in December, both published in *The Watchman–Examiner: A National Baptist Paper.* Bonhoeffer comes to Union and Abyssinian.

1931 Responds to H. L. Mencken's criticism of African–American clergy, "Dunghill Varieties of Christianity," which the Urban League magazine, *Opportunity*, publishes February, 1931. From a sick bed, down with the flu, Powell pens "H. L. Mencken Finds Flowers in a Dunghill," which *Opportunity* Publishes March, 1931. Bonhoeffer returns to Germany.

1932 New York Republicans nominate Powell to serve in the Electoral College, speaks widely in Hoover's campaign as a Progressive Republican, *American Business World* publishes editorial in support of Powell, October, 1932. Junior graduates from Columbia with M. Ed. Powell joins Neighborhood Improvement Club, part of the Democratic Party, supports Franklin Roosevelt's implementation of cousin Theodore Roosevelt's political program, freely criticizing F. D. R.

1935 Tries to retire from Abyssinian at 70 years of age; congregation rejects resignation, so he takes the winter off, leaving Junior in charge, a bitter pill for many to swallow. *The Amsterdam News* publishes "The Silent Church."

1937 *The Watchman–Examiner* publishes "The Negro's Enrichment of the Church Today." Successfully resigns from Abyssinian, which makes him Pastor Emeritus, gives him an un–

precedented pension for life; the church has 14,000 members. Preaches farewell sermon, "Twenty–nine Years Ago and Today."

1938   Publishes *Against the Tide*, his autobiography, fills retirement with political action to end racial discrimination, expand employment opportunities and equal rights for African–American women and men.

1939   Publishes *Palestine and Saints in Caesar's Household*.

1941   *The Watchman–Examiner* publishes "Tolerance in Race and Religion."

1942   Publishes *Picketing Hell–A Fictitious Narrative*, his theo–logical biography.

1945   Publishes *Riots and Ruins*. Hitler executes Bonhoeffer.

1946   Powell marries Inez Means, a Nurse.

1949   Abyssinian publishes Powell's history, *Upon This Rock*.

1951   *Negro Digest* publishes his last article and the only one that is not a sermon first, "Rocking the Gospel Train."

1953   Powell dies.

From Powell, *Against the Tide*, Samuel Dewitte Proctor, "Adam Clayton Powell, Sr. (1865–1953)" in Rayford Logan and Michael Winston, Editors, *Dictionary of American Negro Biography*, 501 and "Powell, Adam Clayton, Sr. (1865–1953)," in W. Augustus Low, Editor, *Encyclopedia of Black America*, 702f. Also, the Clayton Powell, Sr. article on the Schomburg Library's Internet Website of 2002.

Chapter One

A Prophet of Liberation

One year before the Brown vs. Topeka, Kansas, Board of Education Supreme Court decision ended legal racial segregation, a man died at eighty–eight years of age. He spent his life preaching the gospel of Jesus Christ. As a progressive leader, A. Clayton Powell, Sr., was a prophet who led to the 1954 decision. How may I introduce him more than forty years later?

The Powell Chronology (xv–xxi) traces the significant events and publications of his life. The Bible was always important to him, not because he was a literalist, Fundamentalist or Pentecostal, but because he found there what a Spiritual celebrates: "On every page was liberty." As notes the Chronology, he was only seven years old when his stepfather gave him a copy of the Gospel according to John. The branded ex–slave, a dirt–poor tenant farmer, promised to send him to school after age twelve if he could read the Gospel by then. The precocious child read the Fourth Gospel aloud to his surprised family that day, his seventh birthday. Nothing stopped him from reading the Bible except the teenage years he spent imitating the mischievous figure in the pulp fiction series, *Peck's Bad Boy* by George W. Peck, which became a series of movies starring Jackie Coogan. At Howard House, while at Wayland College and Seminary, he read the Bible through. Of his knowledge of the Bible, he received compliments. His ability to season his lectures and sermons with appropriate Biblical material set him apart from Liberals. He never twisted the text to suit his topic; he twisted his topics according to his texts, basing progressive adaptation by the church in changing contexts on the actions of God to which the Scriptures attest. (Powell, *Against*, 21–39, Powell, Jr., *Adam by Adam*, 3).

In The District of Columbia and at Yale in New Haven Powell read the Abolitionists: Frederick Douglass, William Lloyd Garrison and John

Brown. The New Haven African community was a powerful, liberating force locally and nationally. Powell was not the first conservative pastor from the South whom the New Haven community radicalized and activated. Students from Yale Divinity School attending his church played a significant role in helping shape his future. He delivered, sold and published copies of lectures on the Abolitionists in southern New England and across the nation.

Frederick Douglass was the most influential Abolitionist for him. They both loved the religion of Jesus Christ the savior of sinners. Douglass, an African Methodist Episcopal Zion lay preacher, wrote that he believed in the religion of Jesus which comes down from above in God's wisdom, pure, peaceable, gentle, easily accessible, full of mercy, good fruits and lacking partiality and hypocrisy. His religion, Douglass and Powell believed, sends disciples to bind up the wounds of the man besieged on the road to Jericho in the parable of the Good Samaritan. Jesus calls disciples to visit orphans and widows in afflictions, enacting the principle of love to neighbor and God. They hypothesized that if one requires freedom for oneself, one cannot deny freedom to another. Powell followed Douglass's dogmatics in this regard; both men loved Jesus' religion and hated Fundamentalism, which held slaves, closed minds, abused women and destroyed souls. His first published oration was, "The Religion of Frederick Douglass," in 1902. I believe the core beliefs, or dogmatics of this article should be in all anthologies of African–American religious, cultural and social history and all studies of the history of Biblical interpretation in U. S. history. Moreover, this article helps Bonhoeffer scholars comprehend the strong content of Gospel preaching that attracts him to Abyssinian Church with Fisher (In Powell, "The Religion of Frederick Douglass," *The Colored American*, Boston: April, 1902, 339–343, also Philip Foner in Jacqueline Grant, "Black Theology and the Black Woman," in Gayraud Wilmore and James Cone, Editors, *Black Theology: Documentary History, Volume 1,* 331.)

Douglass interpreted Biblical texts through a hermeneutics of descending Revelation from James 1.26f; Luke 10.25–37, First Corinthians 13 and Matthew 5–7 (The Sermon on the Mount, important to Bonhoeffer). His idea of liberty probably entailed Galatians 5. In any case, the hermeneutic goal of reforming the false, slave–owning church according to the religion of Jesus in the Bible was the authoritative charter of liberation. Douglass's hermeneutics took root in his ministry as a lay preacher in the African Methodist Episcopal Zion Church. He wrote of indebtedness to William Serrington, Thomas James, Jehill Benan and Christopher Rush of the A.M.E. Zion Church. Licensed to preach in 1839 by the Quarterly Conference, from the Zion Church he started his Abolitionist career, continuing his relation to Zion well into his career (from Lenwood Davis, "Frederick Douglass as an A.M. E. Zion Preacher," *The A.M.E. Zion Quarterly Review,* October, 1996, 61, from James Walker Hood, *One Hundred Years of the African Methodist Episcopal Zion Church,* 541f.)

Douglass's work anchored Powell's criticism of the hermeneutical options to which he was exposed, while many African–American clergy after the Civil War succumbed to cheap grace Fundamentalist or Liberal European–American Christianity. For example, like Douglass, he advocated the equality and freedom of women, while most clergy, European– and African–American, went along with the male–superior interpretation of Genesis 1–2. James Cone provoked controversy among African–American divines when he noted the same problem in the 1960s and 70s. The passion for freedom of such leaders as Douglass and Powell replaced innocuous, irrelevant diatribes against such non–sins as dancing, smoking and drinking, while ignoring present injustices. They favored pie–in–the–sky, pre–millennial Fundamentalism of European–Americans (Cone, *Black Theology and Black Power,* 105). Fundamentalist interpreters disillusioned him early. They ate more stolen chickens and drank more liquor with less moral compunction than he (*Against,* 13). After his conversion and call to ministry, he tried to live up to high ideals and opposed the cheap grace of such preachers. He was not self–centered. He practiced a Spiritual Biblical hermeneutics from the Spirituals that included a belief in education and always a sense of transforming the world, not just himself, his church, his people or his nation. From New Haven onward, Powell dedicated himself to liberating and empowering women as well as men, one of the strongest aspects of his career, and one previous Powell scholars completely overlooked.

At Wayland, he resolved to help someone every day. Not doing a good deed at the end of one day, he dressed and left the dormitory after 10PM, against the rules, especially for a dormitory proctor such as him. Meeting a ten–year–old girl who lost her father, whose mother had a two–month–old baby, he gave her his last dime. He told that story in 1938 (*Ibid.,* 24). He came to New Haven/Yale already in debt to post–Civil War African–American leaders: Douglass, Bruce, Langston, Lynch, Revills and Pinchback (*Ibid.*) A European–American, former Civil War Chaplain, Maine native and Brown graduate, George Merrill Prentiss King, founded and was President of Wayland, which later merged with other African schools into Virginia Union University, Richmond.

He was Powell's first New England influence and mentor. He came to Wayland a few years after King was accused of physically abusing African-American women (Evelyn Brooks Higginbotham, *Righteous Discontent: The Women's Movement in the Black Baptist Church, 1880-1920*, 52f and note 13, 246). His praise of King's Christian character may mean he was unaware of the charges African pastors in the District of Columbia brought against King. Maybe he was aware and expressed criticism obliquely. He often stated that while European help was appreciated, it was bad for them and worse for African-Americans. Such charity had to end after equalizing justice occurs (*Against*, 181). In any case, His attitude toward women was liberating and empowering, never abusive.

Powell lifted up African-American leaders he felt struggled for freedom and power. Bruce was a Reconstruction era Senator from Mississippi; Lynch, a Congressman from Mississippi; Revills, from North Carolina and Pinchback was governor of Virginia. John Langston was important because he developed a Reconstruction program shared by Progressives of all races. From his work, Powell defined his theological stance as Progressive. Here is the key to understanding the content of the Gospel of Jesus Christ the Savior of sinners that he preached which must liberate us from thinking he or Bonhoeffer were Fundamentalists and move us beyond the emotionalism Bonhoeffer scholars concentrate on, including Renate Wind, Josiah Young and Ruth Zerner (William F. Cheek, *John Mercer Langston and the Fight for Black Freedom, 1829-1865,* 418f). Gatewood criticized early Reconstruction leaders as elitist (*Aristocrats of Color: the Black Elite, 1880-1920).* People had to start somewhere and everyone had blind spots.

After hearing Booker T. Washington speak in Atlanta, the first ex-slave ever to address a predominantly European-American audience, Powell noted, about the speech of his fellow Virginian from the same county, that slavery's chains were off Africans, but manacles remained: Ignorance, superstition, prejudice, intolerance and injustice (*Against*, 39). For the rest of his career, he took manacles off of African-Americans and others. He wove parts of the views of Harris, Kidd, Papini and Durant to shape the progressive, liberating Biblical hermeneutics of the Spirituals, Douglass and Langston. This hones his idea of Progress and sharpens his assault on cheap grace through years of struggle in what he called a world come of age (Powell, "Progress-The Law of Life," *Negro Pulpit Opinion,* January 15, 1928).

Recent studies of Powell focus on his son, who continued but altered his father's agenda. Powell's Biblical interpretation however, evolved in relation to Douglass's religion and Langston's Reconstruction program and changed as other influences changed the community, including Marcus Garvey and Mohandas Gandhi. His concern for the elevation of the masses and not establishing elite agreed with his senior class oration at Wayland (cf Chronology, 1892). Kinney may infer Biblical interpretation by Douglass, Washington and DuBois in such terms as the black tradition or experience, but did not explicate the variety of options in that tradition or experience. Moreover, Kinney, like Welty before him and Clark and Hamilton, mistook Powell for a Fundamentalist or Conservative. None of them mentioned his egalitarian advocacy of women's rights. In their studies of his son, I miss Adam's leadership in passing the law giving women equal pay for equal work. None of them noted his influence on Bonhoeffer. Most critics think he is an arrogant egoist or Fundamentalist, but he was a generous, kind, thoughtful and radical, progressive prophet. (Kinney; Shelton Clark, *Black Clergy as Agents of Social Change with an Emphasis on the Life of Adam Clayton Powell* [Jr.], 1978. A recent study amplified Powell's context: Albert J. Raboteau, *Slave Religion: The "Invisible Institution" in the Antebellum South,* ix.) How did they miss Powell's early article on Douglass, with his criticism of Fundamentalism? How did they ignore Powell's advocacy of women's liberation and equality? Is Powell elitist, as Hamilton maintains in *Dilemma,* 41ff, 46–49, 51, 69, 71–81, 87ff, 145? How was he Fundamentalist and yet received newspaper–published death threats from Fundamentalist groups, African and Anglo–Saxon?

The separation of the sacred from the profane that is traditional in Roman Catholic, Orthodox, some Lutheran and other Protestant Pietistic theological traditions did not exist in Southern New England Puritan tradition or African religion, culture or society unless one of the religions he listed dominated or oppressed. Powell freely criticized philosophy, religion, economics, society and politics, emphasizing the relation between Piety and Progress. Other studies and Asante's work show no sacred–profane dichotomy in Afrocentric hermeneutical options. For example, Powell wrote of King that his actions spoke more loudly than his words, the pragmatics of Robert Browning and Afrocentrism in harmony. (*Against,* 26.) The so–called wholistic world–views among post–moderns were in Southern New England Puritan culture, in Sacvan Bercovitch, *Puritan Origins of the American Self,* 109–135 and in a distinctive view of African religions and cultures by Molefi Asante, *The Afrocentric Idea,* 22–27, 159–195 and others like Melva W. Costen, *African American Christian Worship* and Joseph A. Johnson, *Proclamation Theology,* 30–51. Among European and Latin American proponents of wholism, unfortunately taking the Darwinian line, are Pierre Teilhard de Chardin, *The Divine Milieu* and *Hymn of the Universe,* and Juan Luis Segundo who follows Teilhard. Another advocate of wholism, from a different perspective, was Cochrane, *Eating and Drinking with Jesus,* 8f. Samuel Harris and Powell were ahead of the game in this matter, like Cochrane, Cone and Gutierrez.

Powell welcomed sermon criticism from a Presbyterian graduate of Lincoln University, the first African graduate of Yale Medical School, Isaac Napoleon Porter. The lack of material by Porter prevents any quoting of his views. Powell esteemed his mastery of Immanuel Kant, the dominant force in U. S. academe well into the 20th century. A Consulting Room dedicated to Porter's memory in New Haven Hospital bears mute testimony. Lincoln awarded him two gold medals, in Philosophy and Science. An honorary M.A. followed from Lincoln when he received the M.D. from Yale. He served on New Haven's City Council and died of Pneumonia. Powell mentioned him in *Against*, 31f and earlier wrote about him in, *A Souvenir of the Immanuel Baptist Church and Its Members,*1895. Porter was born in 1865, too. Not imitating *Peck's Bad Boy*, however, he was in New Haven a few years ahead of Powell.

A study of Liberal Arts curricula of the era, 1890–95, reveals the dominant role of Darwinian Evolutionary History, which extolled the supremacy of Anglo–Saxons over all other races in a course all students took: Natural Science. Neo–Kantian, Anglo–Saxon–centered, Darwinian philosophy ruled at the turn of the last century, when the upstart pragmatists, Josiah Royce of California and John Dewey of Chicago, very different, attracted attention. In his context, Powell found Harris, Kidd, Papini and Durant among his most agreeable sources and, after Dewey left Chicago for Columbia, he found Powell a remarkable ally in his extension campus reform, and on the Board of Directors of the NAACP. Kidd, Papini and Durant criticized Anglo–Saxon–centeredness, rationalism, conservative as well as Liberal, and destructive Biblical interpretation. Kidd worked from the standpoint of the new science of Sociology, invented by Auguste Comte of France. Papini rebelled against the romantic idealism of Benedetto Croce, and Durant rebelled against the sublimation of intelligence by the Roman Catholic Church, in dialectical tension with Bertrand Russell's analytical philosophy. Durant held to Dewey's high idea of emotion and intuition. They opened the door for an honest, open interchange between their cultures. Otherwise, the hermeneutic circle shuts to keep out Native–, African–, Jewish–, Arab–, Asian–, Hispanic–, Teutonic–, Italian– and Feminist–Americans.

African–American pastors settled for what was entirely within that circle. One of the biological determinists was Kidd, whose book, *Social Evolution*, 1892, was a typical textbook. His mind changed after World War I and what he saw that Cecil Rhode's men did to Africa. His revised view, posthumously in circulation, *The Science of Power*, frees and influenced Powell.

Powell served Immanuel Church in New Haven until 1908, fourteen years. Then, at forty–three, Abyssinian Church in New York called him. In New Haven, Powell published his first sermon and second article, "The Significance of the Hour," in 1906. He urged people to lay aside denominational prejudices and unite in global evangelism. He established a reputation for broad knowledge and a passion for serving everyone by the time Bonhoeffer was born. He developed a model, or ideal church, by which he reformed the church. Throughout his life, he rejected smooth and placid ways because they ruin people. Along the Mississippi River, we say, "Easy ways make people and rivers crooked." He hated mediocrity. If that made him elitist, so be it. He always tackled big jobs, picked up heavy ends of logs and went after the big fish of racism and poverty. He was a pragmatic harmonizer. This theme, although critical, defined his reputation and enabled him to be a truly prophetic clergyman according to the criterion by which false prophets were distinguished from true, in Deuteronomy 18.15–22. One key was his idea of the simple Gospel. When Powell charged his son to Abyssinian's ministry in 1938, he said the Gospel washes the unclean, feeds the hungry, clothes the naked, comforts the sorrowing, cures the sick and brings eternal life to the dying. The Gospel promise of personal immortality was important to him, too (*Against*, 290). He was consciously part Choctaw and African. Both cultures aim to achieve universal harmony with earth, air, water, birds, animals, self, family, society, culture and other cultures, the cosmos, the spirits. The Spirit will say, "well done," if one brings about harmony where there is dissonance. Unclean = dissonant. Hungry = dissonant. Naked = dissonant. Weak = dissonant. Sorrow = dissonant. Sick = dissonant. Dying is entering into an eternal harmony, the ultimate good news, or Gospel.

Hearkening back to Douglass, Powell harmonized with an historic African–American criticism of a dissonant European–American, slave–owning, woman–beating religion and philosophy. His challenge consisted of whether a progressive, ideal church could make universal, harmonic social change. Could he provoke the church into abandoning xenophobic ways, and apathy toward social problems, to meet the needs of people? Because of Powell's African–, Choctaw–, Christ–like drive toward universal harmony in reality, he truly was a Pragmatic Harmonizer, but spiritually, not materially, determined. The pragmatic philosopher Dewey (1859–1952) highly valued emotion and intuition, and related positively to religion. The difference between African Christianity and European versions emerging throughout this study centers on the influence of Stoicism in the latter, creating a sublimation of emotions and the intellect (in Fundamentalism) and the lack of Stoicism in the former, wherein religious liberating and channeling of emotions and intellect occurs.

Hermeneutically, Powell embraced the intellectual with the spiritual, critical of intellectuals who rejected the Spiritual and conservatives who rejected the intellectual. This study focuses on the hermeneutics of each subject. The hermeneutics Harris stated paralleled his work, not the Existential or Neo–orthodox movements Kinney covered. After all, Macquarrie and Tillich (August 20, 1886), like Bultmann (August 20, 1884) and Barth (May 10, 1886) were born about twenty years after him and many more years after Harris. If K. Barth was existentialist, he belonged in the same category. Strains of thematic development in all the more recent European theologians agree somewhat with him, but his hermeneutics stretched theirs to become more outrageously and radically transforming and reforming of religion, culture and society than they advocate (Macquarrie is Scottish while Tillich, Bultmann and Barth, like Bonhoeffer and others are German, all cultures in which emotional sublimation occurs). He followed and transcended the last of the Federal Theologians, Harris. If academic theologians forget how important Federal Theology is to North Americans of all races, the events following September 11, 2001, remind them. Kinney cared for Macquarrie and Tillich, who came after Powell. He mentioned Niebuhr but omitted his role in bringing Powell to Abyssinian and bringing Bonhoeffer there, too. His use of Harris's Spiritual hermeneutics may have left Kinney with the impression that his view of the Bible was conservative. More conservative than Liberals, yes; less conservative than Fundamentalists, yes! If he was Conservative, why did they publish death threats against him? For Powell, the Spiritual and the Progressive were one idea, that the Spirituals, Douglass, Langston and Harris took from the Scriptures; Progressive, not Conservative or Liberal.

African–American Biblical scholars writing hermeneutics since then, include Joseph Johnson, David Shannon, Vincent Winbush, Itumeleng Mosala and Renita Weems. Moreover, an African–American lay Liturgical scholar, Costen, concerns Spiritual interpretation in the context of African–American liturgical history. She seeks a universal, harmoniz–

ing, pragmatic interpretation of the Bible, such as that of the late Pierre Teilhard de Chardin. African peoples consider reality as one related whole, overcoming the wedge between sacred and secular driven between religion and culture. My mentor, Arthur Cochrane (Cochrane, 8f), also advocated the same idea. Post–Modern theologians who write about the same issue include Peter L. Berger, *Facing Up to Modernity,* Douglas C. Bowman, *Beyond the Modern Mind,* and Harvey Cox, *Religion in the Secular City: Toward a Postmodern Theology,* in Costen, *African American Christian Worship*). They take up a theme K. Barth developed in *Church Dogmatics* (Part I, Volume 1, 36f, 39, 68f, 140, 287f, 295f, 377f, 481, for example). Johnson's *Proclamation Theology* had a similar hermeneutics. A Christian Methodist Episcopal Bishop, holding two doctorates, from Iliff and Vanderbilt, professed New Testament in The Interdenominational Theological Center in Atlanta, the largest African school of theology in the world until his church made him a Bishop; then he died too soon. Unlike Powell, who wrote that he was no scholar, Johnson was. His treatment of Ernst Fuchs' hermeneutics focused on Biblical interpretation as the self–understanding of the text transcended and changed the interpreter's self–understanding (Johnson, 33, 35, 48, 284). He was so concerned with the search for pragmatic harmony that he objected to what he thought was dissonance in Cone's work. Yet, he was more radical in one way than Cone, insisting that the only valid Biblical interpretation, as far as African–Americans are concerned, must flow from the African–American experience (Ibid, 143–152). Powell would find a way to use both points of view, as he did with the Urban League and NAACP, Booker Washington and W. E. B. DuBois, because both Cone and Johnson strove for Progress. He challenged them to free and power women as well as men.

    Powell combined reason with emotion to effect ethical progress. He criticized rationalists' rejection of emotion and emotivists' rejection of reason. Deepening the emotions of sympathy and love made moral progress possible, providing the brain and facts engaged (*Douglass*). This was the position of Harris and Kidd found throughout his work. Welty, Clark, Kinney and Hamilton nowhere said anything about moral progress through emotionalization and Bonhoeffer scholars like Zerner, Young and Wind did not understand emotionalization of the ideal as a well–thought–out, scholarly context and content for mission and ministry (Ruth Zerner, *Union Seminary Quarterly Review*, Josiah Young, *No Difference in the Fare,* and Renate Wind, *A Spoke in the Wheel).* Aristotle advocated control of emotions by reason, but hardly concerned the Greek elites with ethics any more than his mentor Plato. Powell follows the post–War Kidd and Sigmund Freud advocated moral progress through deepening the emotions of love and sympathy. Stoic philosophy held that emotions were problems to solve, not directors of moral action. He believed stifling or suppressing emotions was the problem solved by expressing and deepening emotions to direct moral acts. African Psychology concerned modern Moral Psychologists who agreed with him that liberation of African–Americans entails a confrontation with the dominant, European–American Psychology of control which was more like Aristotle than Freud or his students, Alfred Adler and Carl Jung. Psychological power for social, cultural and religious reformation comes from the truth, power and force of God apprehending us through Bible study, Prayer, Preaching, Baptism and the Lord's Supper. Sanity depending on divine mystery was a position Adler took against Freud.

Powell understands sin as present in all humanity, requiring the divine miracle of Christ–given spiritual regeneration, or justification and acts of will, spiritual sanctification, to overcome. Sin evolves when unchecked by forgiveness and repentance, ending in a tornado of destruction and death (*Against,* 35). He does not mean after death, either, since his goal is to displace the hell in people with heaven now. Take time to read Powell's works and discover that he is never a pie–in–the–sky Fundamentalist. I have no idea where objective scholars get such impressions.

Powell took the church and its critics together. He criticized Liberals who rejected the church and Conservatives who rejected its critics. He criticized the cheap grace of many churches and clergy and the failure to address the needs of what he called, "a world come of age" (62). This phrase came into theology through Comte's Sociology. Comte coined the phrase, Kidd used it, and Powell imitated him. When Mencken assailed the church, however, he rose to defend the church, as the Chronology notes. Mencken's appropriation of Nietzsche was too much for him to abide. He promoted the discipleship and service of the church in harmony, as much as possible, with critics of the church, but he drew the line, with Douglass, Harris, Kidd, Papini and others, at the ideal of Christ–like love. The church provided a great deal of unshackling, ignorance–overcoming education, liberation from superstition, empowering organization and advocacy of the power to overcome intolerance and injustice, in his view. In other words, the church did not sublimate emotion, but liberated people by deepening the emotions of sympathy and love consistent with the ideal of Christ–like love.

Powell subsumed tradition under Progress, rejected Progressives who rejected tradition and Conservatives who rejected Progress, a law of life, a basic principle always in operation is Progress. An authentic Progressive knew when to hold on to the traditional. People who held an extreme position found Powell friendly and difficult, simultaneously. A key statement formed the basis for his assault on all forms of cheap grace and his interpretation of the Bible to a world come of age. He rejected Fundamentalism, Modernism and Liberalism as his class of preachers; he was a Progressive. I ask Powell scholars, is *Palestine and Saints in Caesar's Household,* difficult to read and take seriously? Obviously, the books he published were collections of sermons from decades of work. Only in retirement did he have leisure to write. He never stopped advocating progress, even during his long retirement (*Palestine and Saints in Caesar's Household*, 95).

Powell combined gentle, meek, non–violent love with revolutionary, radical social change. He opposed both Liberal and Fundamentalist rejection of non–violence and Conservative rejection of revolutionary, radical social change (*Upon This Rock* 112, *Palestine,* 152 and *Against*, 192f). This friction divided African–American theologians. On one extreme was Cone in his early days while Johnson was at the other end. Cone's position agreed with left wing Neo–orthodoxy like K. Barth or Gustavo Gutierrez while Johnson's reflected that of right wing Neo–orthodoxy like Bultmann or Teilhard de Chardin and Juan Luis Segundo. African–American interpretations of the Bible and Jesus quickly moved beyond that point, as in two volumes edited by Wilmore and Cone, *Black Theology: A Documentary History*. The same hermeneutical varieties in European Biblical scholarship were among African–Americans. Peter J. Paris described an interesting example of this fact in, "The Bible and the Black Churches," in Ernest R. Sandeen, Editor, *The Bible and Social Reform, 152*. Paris gave a pragmatic explanation of it. Specific perspectives on race relations were more important than the Bible. He noted Pastoral, Prophetic, Reform and Nationalist varieties of hermeneutics (Ibid, 133–152), which fell two types short of Mark Gerzon's social analysis (*A House Divided*). How Powell posited one Lord Jesus for all races and the calling of Africans is a pertinent issue.

Powell combined inclusiveness and reconciliation with an emphasis on African–American unity and power under the Spiritual. He assailed selling out to European–Americans as well as African–Americans' rejecting others, and returning to Africa in their attempt to live free of racism. For better or worse, he thought God entwined the destinies of all races. Developing a better relationship among the human races was a pivotal issue (*Rock*, 52). The interpretation of race relations as an act of God through Jesus included advocacy of African economic nation–

alism more radically than most Establishment African–American clergy of his age. He subsumed the Capitalist ethos under the Spiritual. He subsumed the Entertainment ethos under the Spiritual, not allowing himself to be cast in a Broadway Musical. He subsumed the Patriotic ethos under the Spiritual in his first book, *Patriotism and the Negro*. The Left wing, radical option receives redemption, too, not just the Right. Transformation through Education, however, was the one ethos that he worshiped, but even in education, emotionalization was a key factor. The heart must excite the head and accord with reality if the actions of the student will change for the better, especially the capacity for love and sympathy toward previously hated peoples; only if the learning process receives and follows moral guidance from above.

My study of Powell's hermeneutics also reveals two more factors. He melded the platforms of B. T. Washington, Langston, DuBois and Garvey, under the person and work of Jesus and the Holy Spirit, with a commitment to liberating and empowering women, in my reading of his history. The platform of the Niagara, Canada (American hotels refused to rent rooms to them) Conference in 1909, out of which the N.A.A.C.P. developed, changed his viewpoint. The Platform had eight goals. Free speech and criticism, unfettered and unsubsidized journalism, voting rights for men (DuBois' bias, not Powell's), abolition of distinctions based on race or skin–color, the principles of human brotherhood in practice, recognizing higher education and training as the monopoly of no one race, belief in the dignity of work, a united effort to realize ideals under wise, brave leaders and protest as constant as the problems of racism is the method by which African–Americans will realize and fulfill the ideals of the Platform (Elliott Rudwick, "The Niagara Movement," *The Making of Black America, Volume 1, The Origins of Black Americans,* 133).

Powell constantly wove all eight planks of the platform into his interpretation of the Bible, but never excluded removal of the shackles B. T. Washington spelled out in Atlanta, or his devotion to the full liberation and equality of women. Liberation texts in the Bible, Galatians 3.28 and Colossians 3.11, played a pragmatic role in his hermeneutics. *The Worker* published in Washington, D. C., later on during his ministry, in Harlem, "'The Abyssinian Baptist Church in New York City ... [H]as just gone and done something that no other [African] church in the world has ever done. It hired and paid a young woman, Miss M. Virginia Wood, to direct its young people's work.'" (*Against* 61.)

The Spirituals were the heart and soul of Powell's hermeneutics. Preach ing "The Negro's Enrichment of the Church of Today" at the

Northern Baptist Convention in California in 1937, an article *The Watchman-Examiner* printed, he said words that would thrill the heart of Jean Lasserre. Slanders by the racist press moved Africans to sing their dogmatic theology: "You may talk about me just as much as you please, but I'll talk about you when I get on my knees." He heard orations urging Africans to rise up and wage war against segregation, lynching and the rest of a long laundry list of injustices, but his people sang another dogma: "He sees all you do, he hears all you say, my Lord's a-writin' all the time." When frustration reached the breaking point and pillars of support crumble, said he, another settled interpretation of the Bible sang: "I'm so glad troubles don't last always." During World War One, anti-war meetings frequently we sing the article of faith: "I'm going to lay down my sword and shield, down by the river side, I ain't gonna study war no more." He said his people are more heavenly-minded than any other race; heaven is more real than the cities, like Philadelphia, in which we live. While millions of people lose faith in God and immortality, African theologians believe and sings, "I looked over Jordan and what did I see? A band of angels, comin' after me. Swing low, sweet chariot, comin' for to carry me home." An Anglo-Saxon author, Henry Link, called on people to, "Return to Religion," he said, while Africans never left religion. Like a drunken tenor his friend heard singing in the wee, small hours, said he, we sang, "Halleluiah, halleluiah to the Lamb, all my sins have been forgiven and Jesus made me what I am." While other human races killed enemies in holocausts, his people were commissioned by God to teach the European races, "the meaning of genuine love and sympathy," in which qualities, he claimed, his folk already were superior to other so-called civilized human races, if, as John 1.12f and 29 and Acts 3.6 and Micah 6.8 suggest, anyone who loves was always superior to anyone who hates. Poor in money, like Peter in Acts, he said, "In the name of Jesus of Nazareth, rise up," and, in the words of Micah, "do justly, love mercy and walk humbly before thy God." (*Against*, 273ff, 280f.) The Spirituals interpreted Biblical texts: Luke 6.28, Romans 14.10ff, Job 42.10–16, and Isaiah. 2.4, 2 Kings 2.11.

Powell's Biblical hermeneutics developed in free, joyful connection with a variety of experiences and sources. The hermeneutical principles of Powell I cite in the foregoing derive from my research and not before. They developed throughout his career and not in some neat package at the start, although his interpretation of the Model Church drew from his roots in Douglass and the Spirituals before he met Harris or read Kidd, Papini or Durant. The problem of sin in the interpreting person was real to him, his opponents and the world at large; so was the miracle of redeeming, transforming and saving sinners. Spiritual regeneration affected by the Spirit of Jesus, to which the Bible attests, was a universal event not hinging on a particular set of doctrines. This is a surprising Africanism. His use of Spirituals to interpret the Bible was a basic motif under-girding his opposition to the cheap grace of racist Fundamentalists and Liberals in his efforts to transform the world come of age. This basic theme runs throughout the rest of the book like a bright red thread running through a black tartan.

As one who entered the African-American community through my natural curiosity as a musician and vocation as a Pastor-Theologian, I am aware of approaching this study from outside the discourse's perspective, etically. Asante says Etic criticism comes from outside a culture, while Emic criticisms come from within a culture (Asante, 172f). I do not share his enthusiasm for the nature religions since not a few of them feature needless and cruel sacrificing of birds, animals and people, against explicit Biblical commands ranging from 1 Samuel 15.22 through Genesis 22.1-14 on into the long discussion of the eternal sufficiency of Jesus' self-sacrifice as God's self-sacrifice in Hebrews 10.1-18. Since Powell related to other cultures from the perspective and values of his own, his were what Asante would call Etic criticisms. When a people imagine another culture to be agents of the devil rise up and expect imagination as angels of God, I believe that is a bold, Etic attitude. He rejected the idea that African-Americans needed any more Etic studies. Paris traced the footprints of the four-toed Goliath of European-American belief systems among African-American, and ignored two because he bought into their beliefs. Just as Powell rejected the other two toes of what really was a six-toed monster. The point is that Emic as well as Etic criticism by African-Americans of what Asante calls European-American culture and religion already occurs, just as it occurred a hundred years ago when Powell served Immanuel Baptist Church in New Haven. I do not write this book because I think African-Americans need another study of Powell, but because of my quest for progressive, egalitarian harmony. I want to discover what impressed Bonhoeffer so much that, by studying him, you, with me, will sound like Powell to the older African-Americans of Harlem. Before they all die, I want to remind you of what His distinctive voice says, so you will not fall prey to the fallacy of limiting some of his horizons of meaning to Bonhoeffer's somewhat stunted adaptation. What does his distinctive voice still say? Now I know. Moreover, racism still plagues members of my family, an illness that must receive the healing power of God to cure.

Academe is one place where the most rigid stereotyping still exists. Albert Murray believes the most segregated places of all are the stubborn categorizations of the statistics, studies and surveys of the behavioral sciences (*The Omni–Americans,* 1–15). The same is true for European–Americans, too. As Powell said, if European–Americans hold African–Americans down, they stay down, too. The arena of academic study is a place largely without any sensitivity to African intellectual and cultural elements. Where the tacit assumption is still the old Simon Lagree notion that he battles against all his life–everything white is right and universally true, while everything black (or red, yellow, female, Hispanic or Jewish) is ethnic. Deconstructing racism is an important goal of this book. The racist tendency to paint Powell into the corner of an emotional, African–American, Fundamentalist revival preacher and segregate his influence on the likes of Bonhoeffer to emotion within the racist sublimation of the emotions is overthrown by the facts of his intellectual history. Ruth Zerner and Wolf–Dieter Zimmermann are among the few who seem to comprehend the transforming power of emotion in academic theology.

Powell committed to harmony in the face of powerful dissonance and confusion, including the structural racism inhering within academe. He admitted the possibility of other points of view and interacts openly and honestly with others. Yet, he committed to harmony beyond the scope of neo–Aristotelian or individualistic–phenomenological classifications. I believe he understood the necessity of interactions with Emic (African–American) and Etic (European–American) sources so he could move beyond structuralism and de–structuralism to a pragmatic harmony which is not entirely dissonant with Asante (Op. Cit., 173). In a way, I heard in him an echo of Alyosha's voice in Fyodor Dostoyevsky's *Brothers Karamazov*, "We must love life more than the meaning of it."

This is Clayton Powell, Progressive Prophet of Liberation, from Virginia and Ohio by way of Wayland–Virginia Union University and Yale Divinity School, a prophetic, liberating interpreter of the Bible. Before his time–the way we describe prophets. He related to poor and rich alike, and established fully funded positions for highly educated women on equal planes with men through his prophetic, spiritual, interpretation of the Bible, the Gospel and Progress.

Chapter Two

Spiritual Biblical Hermeneutics

Spiritual Biblical hermeneutics, romantically Christ–centered, was the purview of Anglo–American Protestant Scholasticism in Powell's era, whether Old School or New School. Samuel Taylor Coleridge (1772–1834), the English philosopher, defined their spiritual hermeneutics: "In the Bible there is more that finds me than I have experienced in all other books put together." (Harris, *Self–Revelation of God*, 56.) Samuel Harris (1821-1899), Powell's professor at Yale, followed Coleridge in the path of Cotton Mather (1663–1728), making each interpreter a, "manifestation of the Eternal and Universal One." (Bercovitch, *Puritan*, 164.) This tradition underpinned Harris's hermeneutics. Mather and he were among those Harriet Beecher Stowe cited from Mather's *Magnalia Christi, Vols. 1 and 2,* who made her feel that New England soil was holy ground. Puritan heroism was her inheritance, she asserted, by blood and spirit. She believed Anglo–American clergy were, "children of the morning." (87f.) They would bring in the millennial event, when wars and evil end and the world rejoice in God's light (Raboteau, 101, Bercovitch, 152f). Her father was Lyman Beecher, after whom the Yale Divinity School Homiletics lecture series was named and her brother, Henry Ward Beecher, was the first lecturer in the series. When President Abraham Lincoln met the petite author of *Uncle Tom's Cabin*, he remarked, "So you are the little woman who started this (The Civil) War." However duplicitously–since Mather and Edwards own slaves–they sowed the seeds for the abolition of slavery (109). Raboteau cited Mather's favoring Christianizing Africans using the one blood argument. At their (his slaves') request, he established the Society for Negroes in 1693 (Costen, 30, 142f). Powell referred to the one blood argument in his interpretation of Acts 17.26, John 17 and Matthew 22.39. God made us of one blood, so barriers dividing peoples cannot endure. Artificial, they negate the principles of Jesus in his prayer for unity (John 17) and law (Matthew 22.34–40) that loving our neighbor is the second greatest law of God (*Against*, 192f). Mather's Society was the first Christian organization of Africans in the Colonies. Spiritual interpretation played a role in abolishing slavery and segregation, which made it attractive.

Powell studied under Samuel Harris (1814–1899) at Yale Divinity School, 1895–96. He is the least famous of Powell's sources today. Fifty–seven years old when he came to Yale from the presidency of his baccalaureate alma mater, Bowdoin College, he published four large volumes of theology after age sixty–nine. Roland Bainton noted that Harris was more of an academic theologian than any of his predecessors (*Yale and the Ministry*, 169–173). He entered Bowdoin College at age fifteen, studied under Longfellow and became proficient in literature, German, French, Italian and Spanish. He graduated from Andover Seminary in 1838, received ordination to Congregational ministry in 1841 and served two parishes before teaching theology at Bangor Seminary, from which he went to Bowdoin and, later, Yale, in 1871. Harris did not belong to one particular brand of theology, but departed from them all, in the non–conformist tradition of the Puritans. He took his own path. He posited an intuitive epistemology. Intuition had five powers, to apprehend the true, the right, the perfect, the good and the absolute. During the Civil War, Harris delivered inspirational sermons in support of the Union and the abolition of slavery. Bainton wrote that Harris was the last Federal Theologian blithely confident in that faith of Harriet Stowe that equated the Kingdom of God with American culture (173, 198). An excellent lecturer and preacher, whether speaking from a text or extemporaneously (which he did frequently because of myopia), he spiced lectures and sermons with vivid illustrations from literature, poetry in particular. The millennial event proving Anglo–Saxon superiority for him, the Civil War, ended less than a month before Powell's birth (Twenty–five days after, *Against*, 6). The war changed African–Americans, whose freedom was at stake. Both sides involved African–American soldiers. Early efforts to provide higher education by legions of Puritans and Quakers empowered free Africans. The apparently polarizing, opposing hermeneutical sides acted powerfully in Harris's and Powell's era. Liberals and Fundamentalists played off one another to create a heroic Conservative (Homeric) or Liberal (Dionysian) hermeneutics, as Frederick Sontag and John Roth document in "Secularism as a Religious Context: America Come of Age" in their *The American Religious Experience*, 1–28). They used Spiritual hermeneutics to interpret the future of America in the 1960s. No one of Harris's generation excelled him in positing Spiritual hermeneutics in an international theological context.

Harris favored Martin Luther's idea of each Christian as his own interpreter. The best interpreters of the Bible were persons the Spirit, through the text, interpreted. Biblical texts justify and sanctify all of a person's reasons, emotions and actions (Ibid, 285, 374, 380–385 and *Puritan,* 28 and 109–135, also in Cone, *Speaking the Truth,* 1f, and Costen, 13ff and 17–21). Frederick Whittaker noted that Harris believed the Bible contains supernatural revelation, which was central to his theology, the source of the revelation of God's actions. (*Samuel Harris, American Theologian,* 71f, 77f and 175f.) Most supporters of authoritarian interpretation cite 2 Tim.3.14–17, but, as Harris and Powell protested, everyone who belongs to God through faith in Jesus may learn from the Hebrew Scriptures and interpret them to teach, reprove, correct and train people in righteousness, not assert authority. That his emphasis on the Bible attracted Powell is a fact, or else he would not read Harris so many years later, in Harlem, when Ferris visited him. Because of Powell's interest in the Bible (chapter one) and the Bible-centered historical hermeneutics of the African-American Spirituals and community, anyone discovering the pragmatic, liberating message of the Bible may sound like him. David Shannon found that experiencing God before reflecting on God occurred during slavery and emerged as a paradigm in both Testaments. (Shannon and Gayraud Wilmore, *Black Witness to the Apostolic Faith ,*7 and his *The Old Testament Experience of Faith,* 15fff.)

Blending intellectuality with spirituality in Biblical hermeneutics was nothing new for Harris or Powell. This American hermeneutics differed from contemporary European counterparts like Johann Albrecht Bengel who posited a correlation of spiritual, inner light in the interpreter with the meaning of the Biblical text, but without any practical realization. Bengel was the last of a kind in European hermeneutics, according to Hans Frei (*The Eclipse of Biblical Narrative: A Study in Eighteenth and Nineteenth Century Hermeneutics,* 177–178). Bengel was no slave or tenant farmer, much less African, but a rich prelate of a State Church. Powell was unique, however, because of his African hermeneutics. Not surprisingly, his three rules for Bible reading included reading the text through, not the whole Bible. His hermeneutics changed from trying to read through the Bible, the way one would read a novel, to allowing the message of a text of the Bible read through him. Like Harris, he thought the text must transform the reader. Praying in the Bible was another rule, the familiar classic Spiritual discipline of making the words of the text a personal prayer, so the spiritual food of the Bibles nourished the interpreter. Finally, he passed the message of the text which transforms him on to someone else. (*Palestine,* 206.) The truth the Bible reveals brings, "'irresistible evidence of its having proceeded from the Holy Spirit,'" to Coleridge (Harris cited him) as God finds us in Bible reading, where the Spirit moves our spiritual being in the profound depths of our souls (*Self–Revelation,* 56.) Therefore, Powell said the Bible converted the soul, the Spirit penetrated and changed the soul, cultivated the mind, the highest kind of learning. (*Palestine,* 200.)

The Holy Spirit was God for Harris and Powell. In fact, for Harris the Holy Spirit made everything good, holy and righteous happen. The Spirit was responsible for missionary success (Whittaker, 88). The Spirit created the Church (108). The Spirit reconciled the world to God in the person and work of Jesus (112f). Genuine Progress was the work of the Holy Spirit (154f). Harris emphasized the role of the Holy Spirit in every arena of social progress. Powell's sort of interpreter wove together the Holy Spirit, the Bible, Jesus, intellect, emotion and experience. Raboteau observed that Africans, true to ancient cultural and Biblical traditions, think supernatural, divine actions constantly occur in past, present and future lives. (*Invisible,* 250.) The boundaries of time and space no longer exist in the Spirit of God.

Fundamentalists' theory of mechanical inspiration was deficient, in Harris's view, confusing revelation with the book itself. God's actions, centering in Jesus, redeem us from sin, establish us in God's realm of righteousness, peace and joy in the Spirit, which was the inspired part of the Bible for Harris. The Bible was not God's revelation, but preserved the reporting and interpreting of God's actions in the history of Israel and the Church. (*Self–Revelation,* 457, a view Barth took up in the next century.) The Bible's best interpretation, he wrote, goes beyond the positive errors of doctrines, precepts, religious sentiments and experience when the interpretation reports God's historic actions redeeming people from evil and reveals God's righteousness and grace. (464.) The shift from cognitive to experiential in philosophy provokes the shift to God's actions that the Bible proclaims. Dry–as–dust, rationalist commentaries provide grammar, archeology and the like, but not the Bible's real importance. (109.) Powell wrote that the Bible contains divine revelation, not only such aspects as astronomy, biography, botany, eloquence, geology, history, poetry, rhetoric, tragedy and zoology which its clauses, phrases, sentences and words communicate in the world of literary criticism (*Palestine,* 199).

Harris posited seven arguments against Fundamentalism. Generally, he objected to literalism and a verbal, disintegrating interpretation. (*God, Creator of All Vol.1,* 10.) He opposed mechanical verbal inspiration for implying that divine revelation does not consist primarily in what God does–redemption from sin and developing God's realm–but in telling truths and the moral and religious precepts of inspired prophets. (92.) Powell said Scripture attests to God's interventions in history through the person and work of Jesus. Beyond expecting God's words, the ultimate aim of Bible reading for Powell was to see the face and life of Jesus so he could do his best imitation of Jesus. (*Palestine,* 151.)

Fundamentalism rationalized slavery through a literal interpretation of the Kingdom of God in the Bible, Harris wrote (*God,* 92). This set the stage for Jean–Jacques Rousseau's (1712–1778) rejection of Christianity. Powell came from a tradition within Christendom different from the European and European–American branches in two respects. The African church, he told H. L. Mencken and the rest of the public, was the only church that always opposed lynching and always preached that all peoples are one family ("H. L. Mencken Finds Flowers in a Dunghill," March, 1931, *Against*, 251).

Harris's third argument against Fundamentalism assaulted their notion that divine revelation stopped with the ascension of Jesus and the death of his disciples. He rather posited open–ended divine revelation (*God,* 93). God continuously influenced people through truth, law and love. Reflecting open–ended faith, Powell thought he did not know enough about God to predict how long God will take human evil and act decisively; staying within the eschatology of Jesus in the Gospels and not going beyond it like pre–millennial Fundamentalists (*Riots and Ruins,* 41).

Harris countered positivism, agnosticism and materialism, which he traced to Auguste Comte, throughout his career (Whittaker, 56). He agreed with Comte's emphasis on intuition and emotion while opposing his socialism and empiricism (74 and 102). Keep the name of Comte in mind because there are many more reasons to refer to the father of democratic, secular humanist Sociology and philosophical positivism throughout this book. In Harris's criticisms of theologians and philosophers, he tried to build in safeguards against irresponsible subjectivism in Biblical interpretation, especially that which happened in Fundamentalist circles. Timothy Weber had those in mind who followed Harris's and Powell's thinking, unaware of them, when noting that many associate Fundamentalism with a paranoid style, right–wing politics, closed–mindedness and dogmatism (Timothy Weber in Hatch and Noll, Editors, *The Bible in America: Essays in Cultural History*, 101). Well, duh! Anglo–Saxon Fundamentalism favored slavery, lynching, African–American holocausts across the nation in Harris's and Powell's experience. Powell noted a newspaper report of the Fundamentalist mob in Maryville, Missouri affecting an African–American holocaust and lynching. Theodore Dwight Weld documented abolitionist interpretation (*The Bible Against Slavery*, 1938) while Howell Cobb documented pro–slavery hermeneutics (*Scriptural Examination of the Institution of Slavery in the United States, With Its Objects and Purposes*, 1856). Harris experienced the so–called breakdown of the evangelical consensus among European–Americans to which Weber and Hatch referred as pitting Fundamentalists against open hostility to the Bible against Liberal perplexities about the role of the Bible in the modern world (*Bible in America*, 11). Bainton said he carved out a unique pious–moral interpretation during a traumatic time in Anglo–American history. Powell followed a similar pious–moral route, adjusting his thinking to challenge the Darwinian Sociology as Kidd interpreted it rather than hanging on to Francis Bacon's scientific categories. When Harris and Powell considered Spiritual interpretation, they rejected rigid, Baconian, Fundamentalist categories in favor of potentially flexible, progressive, Darwinian categories. That enabled them to explain and tolerate dissenting points of view while debating them, unlike the monistic versions of Fundamentalist and Liberal hermeneutics (116). Only James Gray, William Evans, Reuben Torrey and John Straton were Progressive Fundamentalists and had little influence in the South that I know about.

The Bible was a charter pf social liberation for Powell and other African–American preachers. Generally, the same was true of all Christian, Jewish and Islamic oppressed groups in North America (Ibid, 9). A Spiritual that inspired the Civil Rights struggle from Abolition days included the line, "I had a little book that was given to me; on every page was, 'Liberty!'" A Swiss immigrant professor who also held that view of Scripture was the late Markus Barth (*Conversation with the Bible*, 1964); after teaching in the Universities of Dubuque and Chicago and Pittsburgh Seminary, he returned to Basel and then to parish ministry, where he organized reconciliation trips to the Middle East until his passing. The Bible was the book that the Spirit of liberty best interpreted.

Powell was not as optimistic as Harris about moral progress through American Capitalism. He believed in a more radical eschatology, a sudden, miraculous occurrence, the result of a careful reading of the Gospels. He thought the world will grow worse. The nations of Earth become the kingdom of the Lord when a new manifestation of Jesus Christ occurred. The next transformation, he thought, will be sudden, like a lightning flash (*Against*, 141).

The First World War and the Great Depression ended all historical positivism, as oppression continued in African–American experience. The economic limitations of Fundamentalism ended, to which Harris objected. He posited political progress through progressive revelation by spiritually transformed Capitalists (*God, Vol.1*, 96). Powell, on the other hand, noted Garrison's rejection of the church because Biblical economics favored slavery (*Against*, 141). Harris's Spiritual revelation experiences, and African slaves like Douglass, contradicted the texts of Scripture that authorize slavery, and any Fundamentalist or forensic interpretation. Raboteau noted that slaves distrusted Anglo–Saxon interpretation and wanted to read the Scriptures for themselves. Their reverence for the Scriptures moved ex–slaves to flock to the new schools, colleges and seminaries in the wake of the Civil War (Raboteau, 239f). More at Yale than at Wayland, Powell found sympathy for the ambivalent eschatological struggle. Raboteau wrote that while a Spiritual assertion like, "I am bound for Canaan's land," meant escaping slavery for Douglass, it also meant going home to the Lord (247). After all, going home to be with the Lord was the last stage on the road to freedom for the authors and editors of the Scriptures, Powell, Harris and, after six months in Harlem while residing in a Nazi prison, Bonhoeffer. Powell practiced the dogmatics of the Spirituals as Douglass interpreted them, not alone, as his predecessor at Immanuel, like him, preached, "'Grace, grits and greenbacks' rather than 'jasper walls, golden pavements, and mansions of Heaven,' emphasizing 'homes on earth, facing upon improved streets.'" (In Robert Austin, *New Haven Negroes, A Social History*, 169.) From Biblical eschatology, he derived future promise and present demands (*Against*, 141). His work prepared people not to die, but to live (*Palestine*, 107). Not yet over, as dissonances attest. Douglass interpreted eschatological hope for Powell. When Sojourner Truth was distressed about the Dred Scott Supreme Court decision, Powell recounted that she went to Douglass for advice. He comforted her with the proclamation that God was not dead and slavery had to, "end in blood." ("Douglass," 341.) For a sinner, he performed a Funeral, while a, "Home–going," was for saints according to Romans 14.7ff.

Harris emphasized differences between Fundamentalism's evil rationalism and the Biblical God–living, loving and energizing people (*God, Vol.1*, 99). Powell agreed with Harris's use of Blaise Pascal's (1623–62) wager, betting his life that there will be a future accountability before God, while not accepting the Catholic context and content Pascal defended with the wager. Nonetheless, Harris's and Powell's rebellion against Fundamentalism was directly through agreement with an amalgamation of Pascal with Rousseau and others who advocate intuit–

ion over reason (*Palestine,* 169). They contrasted Spiritual with rational interpretation to preserve the authority of the Spiritual over the Material, not anti–intellectually, but to effect justice, freedom and joy by holding Capitalism accountable to the strain of Biblical economics that liberates the poor and elevates the masses. They opposed the Fundamentalists' fixed, concrete theory of Truth which arrested intellectual development in favor of a transparent conception (Compare *God, Vol.1,* 98). Powell fully embraced the education theory of his New England mentors. King penned that education always helps people help themselves, that industrial education, as advocates such as Booker Washington taught, diverted attention away from the fullest development of potential through the liberal arts (Refer to G. M. P. King's reports in *The Baptist Mission Home Monthly,* April, June, 1880, March, 1885 and March, 1887). DuBois took the same position in Niagara Falls, Canada in 1909.

Finally, Harris argued that the Fundamentalist theory of verbal inspiration led to petty legalism and allegorizing proof–texting. Against rationalism he posited an epistemology of intuition the Holy Spirit inspires, the Scriptures informs (Op cit, 98f). He posited progressive revelation. In the Holy Spirit God reveals new truths (109). Modern civilization, meaning Anglo–Saxon Protestants, had the main character of a derivation from the Biblical Gospel of the kingdom of God. (Refer to his *The Kingdom of Christ on Earth: Twelve Lectures*, 2.) He asserted a progressive opening of heaven's light and glory, the wondrous love of God, on all the nations, increasingly in the future (111). Justice for the poor and oppressed was a basic part of progressive revelation (*God, Vol.2,* 129). He dismissed Gotthold Lessing's notion of a ditch, broad and ugly, between Biblical and modern historical epochs, in favor of the Spirit transcending historical differences on the basis of *analogia fide* and the sameness of the conflict between the devilish and the divine in the middle of which Jesus, "lived, suffered and died." (Op Cit, 129.)

Authentic Christians were free, spontaneous and joyous because of God's energy which always worked to quicken and convert people from selfishness to faith and love. (In his *The Kingdom,* 2 and 4). Some contemporaries were scientific, rationalistic, self–sufficient in the arrogance of virtue, especially philanthropy, utilitarian, realistic, selfish, intolerant, prejudicial, envious and jealous in his opinion, with no interest in the supernatural or belief, nor humble and honest about sin, not spiritual or sensitive to sentiment and enthusiasm (63, 65 and 238). He equated spirituality with doing justice. Powell asserted the same dynamics of conversion in his interpretation of 1 Peter, said the change in human nature is possible through humility (*Against,*155, 143, 1 Peter texts references: 1 Peter 1.2–9, 13ff, 22f, 2.1–5, 9–17, 3.13–18, 21f, 4.1–19, 5.2–11). The Bible taught him, before and during the Depression, that God is as interested in bodies as in spirits, the Gospel saves souls but also changes the social conditions in which bodies exist (*Palestine,* 95, 182). He experienced the Spirit, not just in Church, but in the world. During the Harlem Renaissance and the Great Depression, Garvey changed African–American psychology more than World War I. Harlem became a symbol of liberty and a land of promise (Op cit, 71). During the Great Depression, Spiritual interpretation was in his preaching. All the time he heard Jesus repeating Matthew 25.34ff. He prayed for God to do what he realized God already told him what to do nineteen hundred years ago (196). He preached and wrote for other African clergy to give a week's salary to meet the needs of the impoverished masses in, "Lifting Up a Standard for the People." Thirty–seven negative and three positive responses appeared. Either the negative preachers, including an African–American Fundamentalist cadre, knew not the Scriptures they pretended to value so highly, or refused, intentionally, to acknowledge its authority in caring for poor folk (230).

Harris wrote that the most important human capacities, theologically, were the spiritual susceptibilities through which the divine influence touched and sensitized us (*Self–Revelation,* 4). Powell differed, rejecting Humanism, and asserted that people were not naturally good. While we may have a spark of God, Ultimate Reality, in us, we were also full of the devil. God waited to give the Holy Spirit, not to people Harris called spiritually susceptible, but to empty–hearted people earnestly begging for help, a quite different pre–conversion state than Harris's. (*Palestine,* 144f.) The poor person cried out for God to come and fill his or her cup. Unlike the Anglo–American New England children who grew up learning how to read their very own Bibles. Unlike the students at Finkenwalde whose teacher, Bonhoeffer, taught them to come to the Scripture empty, desiring to be fed, eschewing the so–called spiritual susceptibilities of a morally and spiritually bankrupt German Liberal and conservative Church.

Like Harris, Powell did not appreciate long–faced, sour–pussed Christians. Typically, Powell thought the hopeful, bright side of religion was the best side. The saving power of Jesus saves us, no matter how morally degraded and low we may be (*Against,* 62). Harris, at the height of romantic heroics, wrote that evidence of Christian theism must meet the thinking of the modern age by holding to Kant's thinking that all knowledge, including religion, begins in experience (*Self–Revelation,* 3). The experiences of World War 1 and the Great Depression destroy most all the blithe optimism followers of Harris, Powell wrote, in a moral vein transcending Harris, with William James and John Dewey as well as Kidd after World War 1, that most people cared not for doctrines but seek a practical interpretation of the Spirit of Jesus in our everyday lives (Op Cit, 250), social piety and morality included one another. The problem of blindly patriotic religion continued in both Liberal and Fundamentalist theological circles, however, as current purveyors of this belief system amply attest.

The African–American Spirituals confessed indestructible faith in a liberating Lord which all churches should imitate (273). Through this emulation the church underwent the next Reformation to move beyond the accretions of the 16th century Reformation. Disenchantment with the failure of Modernity concomitant with Capitalism's, people lose faith in natural force theories of Progress, converted to the belief Powell found in Psalm 127.1: "Unless the Lord builds the house, those who build it labor in vain. Unless the Lord guards the city, the guard keeps watch in vain." (*Palestine*, 194.)

Harris worked in critical, international dialogue with Richard Roethe, among others. Roethe, a German, worked within social–Darwinian social–biological determinism, like John Bascom and Juan Luis Segundo and Teilhard de Chardin all of whom held that Biological determinism was the ultimate state of humanity freed by God. Roethe equated character with moral necessity thus determinative, which made God subject to fate (Harris cites his *Zur Dogmatik* in *God, Vol.1*, 137f, among other places). God no longer was that being greater than which none exists for Roethe or Bascom. I am at a loss to understand why Teilhard and Segundo do not understand the Darwinian pitfall that Anthropologists and Sociologists left behind after Kidd's post–World War 1 work which I cover in the next chapter. Roethe objected to divine foreknowledge because it led to atheism. Harris contended that it guarantees human freedom (143). On the level of infinity, he maintained that God's archetypal plan of wisdom and love were the same. On the finite level he posited, however, that God freely changed methods to counter sin (Ibid, 144, which Martin Luther King, Jr. later included in *The Conceptions of God in the Theologies of Henry Nelson Weiman and Paul Tillich*, 1954). Roethe, like Bascom, was thoroughly monistic, not pluralistic like Harris and Powell. In fact, while his aims were moral, Powell's methods sometimes were not (*Against*, 18).

A mechanical, deterministic moralist, Roethe endured a joyless, loveless, arranged marriage. Also, he supported capital punishment. Like many biological determinists in the United States and Great Britain, not always moral (Karl Barth also discussed Roethe in *Church Dogmatics Part I, Vol.1,* 63, 322f, his mechanical morality in *Part I, Vol.2,* 785, and advocacy of Capital Punishment in *Part III, Vol4, n,* 438). In many ways he was similar to Bascom, who scathingly criticized Harris.

John Bascom, (1827–1911), was Harris's strongest Protestant critic. A student of Laurens Hickok at Auburn Seminary, he departed from Hickok's dogmatic rationalism (from *Things Learned By Living,* 1913 and Sanford Robin Robinson, *John Bascom, Prophet,* 1922). He placed all ethical systems under empiricism, subsumes Christianity under Darwinian evolutionary theory, an extreme form of Christian apologetics. Darwin's theory was a divine revelation superceding Scripture in moral authority. The theory of evolution rationally determined Biblical interpretation. His twenty books and one hundred fifty–eight articles were mostly written while teaching in his alma mater, Williams College, New York. He served, 1874–1887, as President of the new University of Wisconsin. He resigned from that post because he favored Prohibition and knew he was at odds with the mainly Teutonic and Nordic politicians of Wisconsin at that (or any other) time. The Bible lost importance for him. Beyond Hickok, he subsumed all religion under rational, social Darwinism in *Science, Philosophy and Religion.* He totally opposed Harris and, by association, Powell.

The sharpest difference between Harris and Powell was the relation between determinism and miracles. Harris thought continuity between the determined and the miraculous existed in intuition. Powell thought a divine miracle was necessary to encounter and change the determined (compare *Self–Revelation,* 5, 56 with "Mencken," 74). After disillusionment with social Darwinism set in for Kidd, his *The Science of Power* yielded a potentially effective neo–positivism for Powell that enabled him to move beyond Harris. He combined Kidd's principles with Harris's spiritual hermeneutics in the African–American Spirituals, and mastered and continued the African traditional homiletics of making Biblical lessons, characters and themes real and full of meaning (Raboteau, 243). Since there was no distinction between theory and practice in Harris or Powell, there was no distance between hermeneutics, experience and practice. The Spiritual interpretation of the Bible immediately related to the experience of the interpreter, immediately compelled the interpreter to enact the message of the text. He took the message of the Biblical text he allowed to go through him directly into action. Rienzi Lemus said (*Against* 311f) that he brought Kidd into the Church without un–churching himself. The energy of the Bible energized an immediate spate of political, social, moral and economic actions (*Against,* 204–246). The African–American Baptist Convention of New York denied any funding for a community center in Harlem to meet the political, social, educational, moral and economic needs of the people in 1918 (208). The majority want people to get religion, not power. With Burroughs, he wanted people to get both, so he went back to Harlem and built the Center (209). That was at the end of the First World War disillusionment and the beginning of the heyday of the Harlem Renaissance. He confined his action to his congregation, the Urban League and the NAACP. Spiritual hermeneutics effected power, according to him. He quoted from Burroughs in 1935, following a riot in Harlem, that the causes of the Harlem riot were easy to see under the heap of injustices done to African–Americans. They were bound to explode after years of patient suffering. If protesting for freedom and justice were Communist, as the Press cried out, then, she asserts, and Powell with her, that the authors of the Declaration of Independence were scarlet. They advocated not abiding injustices after what they called patient suffering. Rob Africans of inalienable rights, corner them like rats and watch them rebel. The anonymous boy tossing the first rock was only the match setting off the dynamite in Harlem's powder magazine (Greenberg, 5 and *Riots,* 30).

Burroughs and Powell shared the same wave–length concerning the oppression of African–American women as females as Africans and by their own men as a major problem they set out to solve. Powell's essays on the important women of Immanuel Church in *Souvenir* were on the front pages of the book, ahead of the men. He echoed her call for an end to the threefold oppression of African women, especially by African men. She wanted to change the tunes being sung to express making slaves of African women. Sing "Nobody Works but Father," but the African wife and mother did it all, carrying all the burdens, which was why some men lacked energy and manhood. The other tune she wanted to stop was, "I Can't Give You Anything But Love." Love alone was not enough to enable a woman to build a home, bear and raise children, not to mention running every worthwhile church, school, lodge, business and social organization (106f). When he quoted Burroughs, he always called her name.

How Powell correlated Spiritual hermeneutics, the liberation of women and ethical progress using Kidd's post–war social analysis, *Science of Power,* is in the next chapter. At this point I insert what Robert Bennett writes to European–American Biblical theologians. The most serious theological work grappling with the meaning of the Bible for today is African–American. In this project, preachers bridge the gap between what the Bible means then and now. The conversation with African–American theology is the most worthy and profitable, in his opinion (in Bennett, "Biblical Theology and Black Theology," in Wilmore and Cone, Vol.1, 190). The revelation of God as liberator of the oppressed through struggles to overcome poverty and injustice is the Gospel of Jesus, not only a message consistent with it, asserted James Cone ("Biblical Revelation and Social Existence," 174; also, Ernst Kaesemann, *Jesus Means Freedom*, 1969, 13). Powell and Burroughs realized that fact many years before Cone's or Bennett's emergence.

The Gospel of God in Jesus as liberator of the poor and oppressed revealed four implications for Cone, which were necessary because of the evolution of the nature of the American struggle after the 1954 Brown vs Topeka, Kansas School Board Supreme Court decision. All Biblical interpretation is social and political because of the nature of the Bible and the interpreter. Both are social and political by nature. The Bible speaks of liberation of poor and oppressed people in history, in the present and in the future. Building on Harris's and Fuchs's notion of the interpreter the Biblical text converts and spiritually transforms, Cone extrapolated that such exegetes act in solidarity with helpless, voiceless people. Such interpreters critically engaged Tradition and traditions to effect progress through obedience to the voice of God speaking through the Biblical text. The Bible always spoke of the liberating of poor, oppressed and humiliated people (Wilmore and Cone, 174). A Biblical interpretation that fails to help others cannot be correct (M. Barth, *Conversation*, 298). Since Cone did not mention the freedom and joy of God's Spirit, he was open to criticism from Harris and Powell. Many Africans and African–Americans objected to absolute Blackness. Johnson objected to his lack of freedom and joy, on the one hand, and absolute Blackness, on the other (*Proclamation Theology,* 144fff). Cone responded with, *My Soul Looks Back* and *For My People: Black Theology and the Black Church*. After mixing for so long, Powell thought Africans just as full of the devil and evil as European–Americans. Both Powell and Cone criticized African–American clergy who exchanged the zeal for liberation for European–American Fundamentalism or Liberalism. Dialectical philosophy or theology, whether of Hegel or other rationalists, was not consonant with the Spiritual, progressive interpretation of Powell or Johnson (In *Proclamation,* 147–152). He felt that Christ's love did not eclipse Cone's anger, nor did the Spirit discipline his hermeneutics (152f). Cone responded to the criticisms that the conversation revolved around how a pragmatic harmony can develop among African–Americans and other oppressed peoples. North American pragmatic harmonizers, James and Dewey, addressed the issue, unlike others. For example, Comte did not believe Africans would adjust to the modern, technologically advancing world, a point at which Darwinian gradualists found common ground in Europe and Latin America: John Stuart Mill objected. He placed Sociology under the other sciences. Comte placed it on top. Thence, Mill favored liberal social and economic reforms in the United Kingdom, with pragmatic philosophers in the United States, especially Dewey.

Responding to Cone in 1977, Johnson posited four principles of interpretation. The first was as radical as Cone's, as he insisted that Scripture commentaries be in African vernacular and emerge from African–American experience. Liberation was the action of God the maker, sustainer and redeemer of planet earth. Note that Johnson places this work with God and not in Christology, as Cone does. Jesus reveals God's power, wisdom and love, actively healing, liberating and reconciling people to God and each other. Jesus' life, ministry, death and resurrection radically transforms the human situation and makes triumphant Christian living possible (Op Cit, 50). Powell, Cone and Johnson agreed that the Spirituals were the dogmatic theology for African–American religion, culture and society. Cone's *The Spirituals and the Blues* was his theology of music, and Johnson gave the highest role possible, just below Scripture, to the Spirituals (39f, 45, 48, 246f, 252, 256f). There was the connecting concept from Coleridge and Mather to Harris, Powell, Cone, Johnson, Hatch, Noll and Bercovitch. Africans receive spiritual food when any interpreter wrestles with the Biblical text to reveal, because of spiritual transformation, that God works in every aspect of life (compare *Proclamation,* 46f with Cone, *Speaking the Truth,* 22–29). The emphasis was on every aspect of life (Costen, 13). Emotional freedom was the issue. Harris placed emotion under intuition in epistemology, the traditional Kantian approach, whereas Powell places intuition under emotion *as* epistemology, traditionally African.

The Holy Spirit, through music, song and storytelling (originally by a Griot, later by the Preacher), was the means forging and flaming the theology of the people. This heritage among all Africans, whether on the mother continent or elsewhere, channeled the Spirit to edify and empower the body of Christ. (Costen, 15.) No epistemological analysis penetrated the freedom of the Spirit moving among human intuition, emotion and reason in creative inspiration any more than twentieth century psychological, sociological and anthropological analyses. Powell's concern in Spiritual hermeneutics to cooperate with a power greater than which none exists to transform her (the interpreter), persons, peoples, places and things according to the wisdom, peace, justice, mercy and love of God attested to by the apostles and prophets of the Bible, the impenetrable core of the creative subject, as mysterious as the creative core of God as Creating Subject in Luther's and Coleridge's interpretation. Further evidence of this factor is found in the next chapter, on ethical progress through emotionalization. He insisted on costly obedience against cheap grace and the Spiritual transformation of people in a world come of age, affecting love and power through conquering meekness. He was an exception to Joseph Washington's ruling that Christians failed to contribute Christian freedom to Africans. Unlike J. Washington, Powell sought freedom from and after the abolition of slavery, like Douglass, and found dignity in egalitarianism before and during the twentieth century (against J. W. in *Black Religion: The Negro and Christianity in the United States*, 1964, 239). Cone and historians of the African churches agreed that Douglass– and DuBois–like clergy advocating liberation were rare, but Washington made the blanket statement that they did not exist at all, laying the blame at the feet of the European–American church alone. The credit for a theology and ethics of liberation belonged, however, to the Holy Spirit and the Bible in the Spirituals and the Spiritual interpretation of the Scriptures by Douglass, Powell and their kind. Among the few European–American leaders who interpreted the Bible comprehensively, insisting that racism is a European–American problem for which they are responsible were: Albion Tourgee, Josiah Strong, Washington Gladden, Walter Rauschenbusch, and Lyman Abbott (in Ronald Cedric White, Jr., *Social Christianity and the Negro in the Progressive Era, 1890–1920*, 1972, 265). As those men died between 1916 and 1920, other European–American leaders joined forces with Powell and other Progressive African–American leaders. Powell, in particular, because, in the words of his son, "'My father was a radical and a prophet.'" (James Blackwell, *The Black Community: Diversity and Unity*, 1956, 5.)

Spiritual Biblical interpretation connected with the psychology of religion in European–American theology, just as psychology in relation to social, cultural and religious spheres always concerned Powell and the North American pragmatic harmonizers such as James. Carroll Wise based *Psychiatry and the Bible* on a presupposition similar to that of the Progressives of 1870–1920. The progress of modern science, he wrote, reached understanding of the causes of illness close to Biblical insights (Wise, 5). Alfred Adler's psychology hinged his work and the works of Barbara Overstreet, Gordon Allport among others. The Biblical revelation was perceivable through faith–guided intuition. He thought the Bible interprets God's life in our lives. Otto Baab's Form–Critical interpretation of the first testament combined with Ernest Saunder's of the second and the Gestalt Psychology of Carl Christiansen and Overstreet. He claimed that neither Psychology nor faith prove or disprove each other (27). Sarah Taggart adopted Gestalt Psychology, thought approvable any religious belief system "that works," without advocating a theological norm, but under a humanist theory of spirituality (*Living as If: Belief Systems in Mental Health Practice,* 1994). Taggart's view was sentimental, not caring what another believed as long as one believed it sincerely. For an example of a Psycho–Spiritual interpretation of therapeutic guidance in the African–American Church, Edward P. Wimberly wrote of a pastor colleague who set an example of open and honest mourning for his congregation by frankly expressing his feelings during a Christian Burial Service (*Pastoral Care in the Black Church,* 62). His interpretation of the Psychology of Carl Jung in his pastoral psychology and care may be as manifestly a political stance more conservative than Cone's as Jung differed from other Psychiatrists in his support of Nazis. He agreed that the Black Theology movement of the 1970s changed African–American psychology from conforming to European–American culture to a distinct psychology, reinterpreting the psychological change effected by Garvey to which Powell referred so positively. He wrote that Black Power and Black Awareness responded to racial integration, rebelled against conformity. In the separatist movement, Africans did not have to be European to be important (*Pastoral Counseling and Spiritual Values: A Black Point of View,* 56–70). He referred to Cone's *Black Theology and Black Power* and Albert Cleage, Jr., *Black Christian Nationalism,* 1972).

Powell and Burroughs paved the way for Wise and Wimberly to access Spiritual Biblical interpretation to free African– and European–Americans from slave and owner mentalities, which resisted freedom (19). The difference between Powell and later proponents was his relating to separatist (radical) and integrationist (conservative) psychologies, sociologies and anthropologies through Spiritual hermeneutics. The complexity of problems were the ways inferiority and superiority feelings created mental and social illnesses (study Adler, "Individual Psychology," in Carl Murtchison, Editor, *Psychologies of 1930, The Science of Living* and *Superiority and Social Interest*). Teilhard asked a rhetorical question at the heart of the matter, in effect, asking if all suffering peoples unite their sufferings so the pain of the world is one great act of consciousness, of sublimation, we would have a most exalted expression of the mysterious work of creation we could ever behold. (*Hymn of the Universe,* 94.) He believed the distance between the rich and the poor was like the distance between the Bridge and Hold of a large Ocean Liner and that the poor in the Hold have little chance of addressing the Bridge, especially given the slow pace of change he associated with Darwin. Powell had no patience in this regard. Following Soren Kierkegaard's eloquent defense of emotions and subjectivity against the rationalism of Hegel in the 19th century, the division between some Continental against some British philosophers on this problem set the stage for World War 1. Nietzsche tossed all Christian moral concerns out in favor of a primitive return to base instincts and the values of courage and power, radically male–centered. His work gave rise to both German war machines, for the first and second world wars. Spiritual Biblical interpretation found a way through the shifting tides. On the one hand all Spirituality disappeared among an entire segment of Form Critics when Rudolf Bultmann tossed everything emotional and miraculous out of the Bible, buying into Heidegger's exaltation of Hegel's idea that nothing is something, so nothing replaced religion in philosophy. Edmund Husserl argued, but to no avail. Shortly after Heidegger escorted him out of the Frieburg University Library on orders from Hitler to expel Jews from the school, he died in 1938 in New Jersey. Max Scheler came to the Catholic Church and then left it because of emotional issues: The Church sublimated emotion under religion, the wrong path to take as he and Husserl viewed human nature. Unfortunately, he would leave my Church, too, as we subsume freedom under order in our Spirituality. They believed love was the cord binding all humanity together, a love of life, whether life seemed to mean anything at all in the mind of any interpreter at all. Hitler suppressed their philosophy and exalted Heidegger's. Powell took the concept of Spiritual Biblical interpretation out onto the battlefield, not just into the marketplace of ideas. Bonhoeffer followed him inasmuch as he followed Jesus Christ the savior of sinners. The path always went in Jesus' steps (1 Peter 2.21–25); the meek method that he knew saved his people, even during the days of slavery when all hopes for freedom seemed to die unborn, as all hopes for justice and freedom died during the reign of Kaiser Wilhelm and, later, the Third Reich. Powell's free Spiritual interpretation created orders to suit the force of the Word, a liberty for which others, like Scheler, Husserl and me, also struggled.

Chapter Three

Ethical Progress Through Emotion

Emotionalization determined ethical progress for Powell ("The Negro's Enrichment of the Church Today," 842). Contrary to him, J. Washington, Jr., 1963, European–Americans withheld autonomous self–criticism from African–Americans so they could not raise ethical issues (In his "Are American Negro Churches Christian?" in *Theology Today, 20,* in *Documentary, Vol. 1,* 95). The Spirituals, Douglass, King and Harris gave Protestant moral self–criticism to Powell in generous doses. Moral progress was a goal for him, personally and professionally. Moral progress through the emotionalization of the ideal was a hermeneutic principle. What did he mean by emotionalization of the ideal if the concept neither excluded nor depended on rational criticism? The ideal about which he set out to emotionalize people was universal love. Feelings of sympathy and love must be deeper, he thought, for moral progress to occur. African people were the most emotional, he said, and therefore able to emotionalize all other races. Especially the more rationalizing and individualizing races, like Anglo–Saxons, needed the help of African people in order to make moral progress. Powell brought Kidd into the church without compromising his integrity as a Christian Pastor, differing from another Kidd–influenced leader, Mao Tse–Tung (in Crook, 176f). One pragmatic–harmonizing result of both men's use of Kidd was equal power for women. He cited Stanley Jones and Kidd as influential advocates of a revision of Comte's concept of the emotionalization of the ideal ("Enrichment," 20, *Upon This Rock,* 115 and Enoch Oglesby, *Ethics and Theology from the Other Side: Sounds of the Moral Struggle,* 1979). Comte placed the moral progress of the masses under the emotionalization of ideals led by emotional people, the most naturally emotional of which were French women, but without the emotional sabotage of religion. Kidd said religion managed to focus religious women on proper ideals. Powell rejected the view that either women or men were superior or inferior to each other as he realized that Africans were more emotional than European women and men put together. The concept among European philosophers of sociology the likes of Comte and Kidd, read through African eyes, became a bridge between the two cultures in the hands of Dewey, Powell and their kind. The clash between the culture of reason and the culture of emotion was already underway by the time Kidd experienced disillusionment and changed his opinion. Who was Kidd?

Benjamin Kidd (d.1917) was a self–educated British Sociologist. He worked in the revenue office of the government until his first book earned enough money for him to leave his job, his life spent traveling and writing. A Darwinian biological determinist in his first book, World War I and what Cecil Rhodes and his men did to Africa disillusioned him. His race was superior to others before the War. He advocated moral social evolution through Anglican Christianity. An instinctive feeling among intellectuals, he wrote, revealed the feeling that a definite stage in the evolution of Western civilization drew to a close, and that we entered a new era, one in which a science of human society, or sociology, was called for to counter the rising tide of Karl Marx's social analysis. Henry Spencer's synthetic Darwinian sociology, formulated following Comte's work, was inadequate. Neither Marx nor Spencer nor Philosophy offered adequate solutions, but only religion (*Evolution*, 1ff). The problems Anglo–Saxon culture spawned developed from the core problem of individualism. The unchanging moral law of progress was unavoidable for him. Theologians were unable to be as direct or emphatic as Darwinian sociologists (viii). The Salvation Army came close, adapting the poor and down–trodden to the religion, culture and social norms of Anglo–Saxons. The major social change Kidd witnessed was educating and empowering of the working poor by the middle class. This social action involved many progressive church people, against whom conservatives (read Fundamentalists) rebelled. His phrases were similar to some of Powell's cited above. The concern of religion for the actual state of humanity in an after–life must change to focus on the present life. So, Powell preached that the purpose of religion was to get the hell out of people and heaven into people in the present moment. Kidd wanted churches to concentrate on what they had in common instead of their differences, so Powell preached Christian unity and worked toward unity throughout his career. The actions of churches were more important than their creeds (almost exactly Powell's words). (14, compare with *Palestine* 107, and Powell, 1906, and *Against,* 30f.)

The preference for the educational valued over and against the religious appeared early on at Wayland in a report by an African-American teacher. His zeal for the scholarship of students surpassed his concern for their spirituality (*Baptist Home,* 1880, 212). Powell celebrated discovery, science, invention, education, free speech, more liberal and objective Biblical hermeneutics revolutionizing thinking and acting patterns. The church was useful to the extent that she adapted to these rapidly changing realities (*Palestine,* 98). His growth beyond an earlier appreciation for imperialism was evident in his reading of the novels of Joseph Conrad and in his changing with Kidd after both men experienced World War One.

The pre-War Kidd, like John Bascom and Richard Roethe, elevated Darwinian sociology to the level of a new revelation from God and the historical-critical study of the Bible from Henry Strauss's very critical analysis to Pierre Renan's romantic-idealistic portrait of Jesus (*Evolution,* 16). Leon Bloy of France reflected Ernest Hello's criticism of French religion, averring that the church tolerated every sort of truth except the liberating truth of the Gospel; he specified Strauss and Renan, as did Giovanni Papini in the next chapter (in Raissa Maritain, Editor, *Leon Bloy, Pilgrim of the Absolute,* 1947). Harris wrote that Darwinian science was a gift of the Holy Spirit, but hardly an exalted divine revelation dominating all of religion (*Self-Revelation,* 6). His view was similar to Powell's. The church must supply social as well as spiritual needs ("The Church in Social Work," *Opportunity: A Journal of Negro Life, Vol. 1,* 1923, 15). Jesus led all Progressives, so anyone who followed Jesus must become a Progressive ("Rocking the Gospel Train," *Negro Digest,* 1951, 11). He struggled against social Darwinians throughout his career, pleading with them that they wait five hundred years before passing judgment on African people as inherently, biologically inferior. During that half-millenium, he called on Anglo-Saxons to give industrial progress and mental development so his people could progress (*Against,* 188).

Through industrialization, Kidd held before World War 1, Anglo Saxons exterminated or subjugated other human races (*Evolution,* 62). They ruled Africans in the U. S. South, he noted, although the ruled were far greater in number than they (52fff). He was on Harris's wave-length, however, in thinking Anglo-Saxons did the perfectly virtuous act of abolishing slavery (49). He did not notice what Powell experienced. Under minority Anglo-Saxon rule, Africans were not free and human in both law and practice anywhere in the South (*Riots,* ix). What was the stage of evolution through which Kidd thought he lived? From rational, individuated self–interest to the level of social creature (*Evolution,* 63). Awareness of the horrible impact of Anglo–Saxon rational self–interest moved him to make the next stage a crusade because the social interest of humanity directly opposed individualism (84). He celebrated the church's supra–rational or emotional–intuitive function in Western civilization. He summed up the function religion fulfilled quite unconsciously parroting the social–rhetorical plot of Aristotle. Working in obedience to the elite class, or the rhetoric of *Movere,* the church as *Placere,* or catechesis, allowed some free play to intellectual forces necessary for the socio–economic functioning of the masses and, as *Docere,* or emotional play, provided ultra–rational sanction for oppressing poor masses (140). Most clergy went along with this program, cheapening the grace of Christ to make poverty and oppression wonderful conditions with which to be content, the efforts of Douglass and Powell stood out in sharp contrast against Kidd's early stance. He believed deepening piety is possible through natural selection (263), but not Powell, who agreed with DuBois, Langston and Garvey what he did in his churches to achieve as much transformation and power as possible, natural selection be hanged. What the daily disillusioning of African–Americans by the terrorism and holocausts visiting them fell on Kidd's awareness like a ton of bricks when he went to Africa and when World War 1 finally felled his naive optimism. Depression led him to rip up a second book he wrote in 1915. He wrote a new one. He died immediately after completing *The Science of Power* in 1918. Kidd saw in England what Powell saw in Germany: they walked away from the Bible. They followed Rationalism. They engaged in a mad rush to conquer and dominate all others. They followed the will to power theory of Nietzsche. Garvey came to Harlem and made Powell feel ashamed of being a light–skinned African–American (*Palestine,* 69, 71, 155f and 192). He changed the psychology of African–Americans from inferiority to equality in every respect. Kidd renounced materialism and moral supremacy, the bases of his earlier work. His people proved they were no better than others. Each race had a special intelligence (*Power,* 117). Civilization rested on emotion, not reason, the secret of the future, he wrote (124). The capacity for emotion described the completeness or wholeness of an individual and a society. His new position sounded like music to Powell. His mentor King believed academe was color–blind, that the arts were not racial; the sciences addressed the mind, not skin color (*Baptist Home Monthly,* June, 1880, 121.) Powell thought the outstanding features of African psychology were sympathy and love, the greatest of the emotions among all peoples, and Africans are the only race with enough love to love their enemies (*Against,* 280).

After the War, Kidd cited Germany's exploitation of the emotion of the ideal to make young men sacrifice themselves in war. A miracle from God would overwhelm and control what seemed an inborn tendency to violence (*Power,* 129–154). The propensity for violence was the ideal under which elite power–brokers subsumed Christian religion (178). The church must serve Jesus, the righteous, gentle, supreme passion for God, wrote the disillusioned Kidd. Jesus transformation was the miracle to free the entire human race from Darwinian Sociology (167f). Divine miracle as power was not new for Powell. With Douglass, the Spirituals, King, Harris and now, the post–War Kidd, he asserted that we were brought into vital contact with the source of all power through faith in God and his son Christ Jesus. Emotion was the greater part of his knowledge (*Palestine,* 145, 123). He knew about miracles from experience. He replied to Mencken's criticism of African–American, dunghill clergy in 1931, when Bonhoeffer was at Abyssinian. That Africans believed any religion or deity of Anglo–Saxons was a miracle. Ignorance actually prevented Africans from cursing God and dying (as a spouse advised her husband in Job 2.9). Comparing the average person of both races, he saw that Africans exceeded Europeans in love, veracity, long–suffering, meekness and patience ("Mencken," 73f).

Kidd's new work posited eleven principles governing a new science of power which actually revived the Positivist emotionalization of the ideal of Comte, as Kidd admitted. The principles of power displaced the dogma of Darwinian sociology as a philosophy interpreting Christianity. His principles influenced power brokers of revolutionary masses around the world, Mao Tse Tung among them (Crook, 176f). His principles consisted of two axioms, three distinctions between force and power and six laws governing the application of the science of power. Truth itself was the science of power and the evolution of life followed maximum power, so force was subsumed under power, which was subsumed under truth, and force was set at the bottom, under power (*Power,* 192).Power, the lowest servant of truth, controlled the social integration of individuals (193). Power was our capacity for using force by integration, producing greater results than otherwise possible. Power characterized life while force characterized materials. Life, a process of integrating forces, followed self–asserting individuals to the greatest social achievements (194). The entire subordination of individuals to the welfare of the whole society projected beyond life, welfare and consciousness of the units an orientation toward the future (195f). No individual could possess the greatest integration of power and determine collective evolution, which was dictatorship, the idea Henry Ward Beecher asserted as much as the Kaiser, namely, that the Pastor was the most highly evolved personality dominating all other personalities. Reason always was selfish while emotion always was other–oriented. The emotion of the ideal determined the science of power (197f). Kidd carried the application of his finding to include Maori women and children, not just Anglo–Saxons, a key divergence from Comte, although he created the word and concept of altruism to define ethics as that which sought the good of the other rather than one's own selfish aims. When this moral ideal became the capacity of a particular race or religion, problems of exclusion arose. The definition of evangelism as self–interest totally misinterprets the Church's altruistic motivation and expression against itself. The spread of altruism required evangelizing Christianity as life required breath.

Heredity was one way the ideal of truth functioned, which Kidd called protoplasmic continuity. Within the life of one generation, however, the emotionalization of the ideal transformed religion, culture and society on a grand scale (198). With Comte, he affirmed that, through the necessities of life, women were more sensitive to the emotion of moral ideals than men. The mentality of women was closer to that of God's mind than the mentality of men, which is incapable of rising to the lofty moral level of emotionalized–idealistic women (240 and 203, 209 and 219). Repeatedly in a variety of ways he asserted the new dogmatics that emotion best conveyed knowledge and not reason (259, opposite Bascom), His new creed was very far from the point at which Bascom wound up. Kidd's creed was the power of the complete expression of the ideal, the science of organizing individual minds in the service of the universal, for truth was the science of power (*Science,* 309). Bascom, on the other hand, said that monism subjects laws of matter to laws of mind and took both up into God (*Things Learned by Living,* 203; other monists included Roethe and later on, Tillich and Heidegger, both of whom proceeded on the basis of Parmenides' monism). Powell resisted monism, whether of the rational or emotive extremes.

Bascom held that the Bible, full of conflicting ideas. and proposed to substantiate whatever truths may be there through a process of hermen–eutics, criticism and philosophy called "mental bias." All doctrines of Biblical authority were out. With the Continental Enlightenment, he thought the Bible as subject to critical analysis as any other literature. Coherence and intelligence was his goal, not emotion, supernatural revelations or miracles. Human nature interpreting human nature was his program (Bascom, *Science,* 39f). Only one way of being human, however, not pluralism, as post–War Kidd and post–slavery Douglass

Powell affirmed.

Powell interpreted the distinctive contribution of Africans to other human races. Jews made religion a national enterprise. Romans made religion an organization. Anglo–Saxons made religion an individual matter. Africans made religion emotional. Persons ignorant of psychology, philosophy or religion decried African emotionalism (*Against*, 277fff). The disillusionment of Kidd (*Power*, Introduction) resonated with the earlier statement of the Pole who became a famous Dickensian critic of Western culture, Joseph Conrad, to the effect that Western conquest mainly means taking the planet way from peoples whose complexions differ from ours and whose noses are flatter, not pretty at all (in *Joseph Conrad: Selected Works*, 1994, 6; on Powell's possession of a complete set of Conrad novels, see Powell, Jr., *Adam by Adam*, 25).

Powell experienced what Conrad and Kidd knew was ugly. He experienced both sides of emotion; feelings that fed mob violence and those that made justice and peace. A righteous rioter of 1943 seemed to him to say, "'Shoot me, I would rather die here for my people than in Germany.'" (*Riots*, 50.) Throughout his career he attacked racism, provincialism and parochialism. He asserted that the world come of age looked for cheery–faced, broad–shouldered people, but even more so for liberal–minded, broad–hearted men. That world was sick and tired of little, narrow, two–by–four men whose interests did not go beyond their families, churches and races (*Palestine*, 185). In Germany, he saw the art on the buildings and was unable to tell any difference between grace and war glory. He was not a pacifist as far as Germany in World War 2 was concerned. Africans fought with the United Nations to beat the notion of a master race into history's dust and Hitler, too. He pledged warfare until Judgment Day if necessary until the Simon Lagree notion of Anglo–Saxon superiority and African inferiority in Harriet Stowe's *Uncle Tom's Cabin*, disappeared from earth (*Against*, 94, *Riots*, 102). Evidently, the cyclical nature of violence eluded him.

Powell, before Kidd, favored equality for women. Any race's destiny was in the hands of its women, a summary of a sermon he preached more than forty times,, "The Molding Influence of Woman," based on Jeremiah 31.22, :"For the Lord has created a new thing on the earth: a woman encompasses a man." (*Palestine*, 177.) He interpreted Genesis three to mean women and men walking together, side by side (*Palestine*, 173). Departing from patriarchal orthodoxy in step with the later Kidd, he asserted that woman was not taken from man's head to be over him, nor from his foot to be under him, but from his side, to be equal to him in the struggle of life (172). Patriarchy was the result of the Fall which was overcome by the blood of Jesus (173f), the universal source of power (229, Matthew 28.18). He addressed themes from Harris, the later Kidd and Papini, who will be met in the next chapter. He asserted that, by being messengers of meekness manifesting the spirit of meek and lowly Jesus Africans preserved themselves under the most trying of situations ("Enrichment," 842). Appropriate power feelings came from the Holy Spirit ("Rocking," 12). The Spirituals were the finest revelations of God outside of the Bible, bringing heaven near the earth and bringing earth to heaven, a simple wording of what he may not have known was the theology of music of another African, Augustine of Hippo (*Against,* 273, "Rocking," 12). The best aspect of worldly existence was emotionalism of a certain ideal ("Give Me That Old Time Religion," *Negro Digest,* 20). In a carefully reasoned attack against cheap grace Fundamentalism and Liberal Hegelian positivism, he contended that evangelism did not depend on the Virgin Birth or bodily resurrection or even miracles, but on the Spirit of Jesus. The Christ idea or Spirit was indestructible, more so than truth, beauty and goodness (*Palestine,* 217). He knew Fundamentalism's stress on the virgin birth, bodily resurrection and miracles of Jesus, but also their angry, violent, lynching and burning objections to the liberation of the oppressed. He studied Liberal reliance on the Hegelian dogmas of history: beauty, goodness and truth. To them, African–Americans were anything but beautiful, good and true. Against those cheap grace options, the power of Jesus came through experiencing God's purifying and rising power (151). An emotional outlet was the greatest gift of the church to African people, who had enough emotion to move earth when directed and disciplined (*Upon This Rock,* 13, 15 and "Old Time Religion," 20). Education provided the directing and disciplining emotional people needed. He worshiped education (*Adam,* 27). Education was a process connecting emotion, intellect and facts for this complete scholar, not a cold, unfeeling, marionette–making.

Multi–racial inclusiveness was the point of power integration in Kidd's scientific sociology of power for Powell. Reflecting Rousseau's influence, he thought Africans were the most forgivable, loving people in America until prejudice, lies and hatred changed their psychology, making Africans as filled with lies, hell and hatred as their oppressors (*Riots,* 36). He appreciated the risks European–Americans took when they crossed the tracks to achieve justice. When a racist Detroit congregation dismissed such a pastor, he noted that a European–American, unprejudiced Pastor could not stay in a racist church more than six months.

Prejudging African–Americans criticized Powell because of his racially inclusive ministry. He boasted of European–, Jewish–, the European–American teacher for the Red Cross School, the mixed faculty in their extension campus of Columbia's School of Education and the German teacher in the Sunday School, although Bonhoeffer was only there six months. He called Clarence Powell to direct reconciliation trips to bring non–Africans to Abyssinian (*Against,* 253 and *Riots* 104 and 135). From 1928 on, Union Seminary students were brought to Abyssinian as part of their theological education (190f). Social change was his mission frontier, as well as for his New England mentors at Wayland/Virginia Union and Yale Divinity. Christianizing society was the Church's paramount duty. The Church must be more spiritual than emotional, because only a Spiritual program could bring about God's social reign and bring order out of our confusion ("The Church in Social Work," 15). He blended the intellectual with the emotional in Spiritual hermeneutics, as taught by Harris in chapter two. Also, individual denominations and races were integrated within the universal Spiritual collective, as Kidd advocated. The collective promoted powerful social, cultural and religious changes. In other words, he did not attempt integration as the absorption of the African into the European, but as changing the European by African culture. Miss that point and misunderstand his hermeneutics, and lose his message.

Carrying out B. T. Washington's liberation from five handcuffs, Powell believed in overcoming ignorance through education and carrying out DuBois's more radical program, overcoming parochialism through inclusion. Both frontiers of progress required emotionalization of the ideal of the universal, meek, strong, humble love of Jesus to affect ethical, multi–cultural change. In this way moral leadership was a major focus. Bainton wrote that morality was part of epistemology for Harris and moral progress was Kidd's major concern. Powell led several moral crusades during his long career (*Against*, 209–220, Bainton, 170). The hermeneutical principle of deepening the emotions of sympathy and love enabled him to crusade against a variety of evils in favor of opposite, constructive, goods. He opposed cheap grace accession to Yale University in New Haven, re–establishing 11:00AM and 7:30PM Sunday services, an act as radical as wresting financial control of Immanuel Church from a European–American Board. Other African–American preachers attended his first 11:00AM service. They expected to laugh at empty pews. Instead, they announced that they will start 11:00AM services the next week after they saw a full house. Against xenopho-bic, cheap grace denominationalism, he instituted pulpit exchanges between Africans and both European and African pastors of congregations of other churches (30f). He said African–Americans were too jealous and undercutting of each other and lacked ambition. He exhorted his people to stand on their own merits (40f). Fellow clergy attacked his ambition and costly obedience. When he built the new church in Harlem, a friendly enemy said he crucified members to make himself famous (73). A prominent real estate broker publicly said that he should be sent to prison (50). He singled out pimps, prostitutes, dive keepers and bookies as sinners needing salvation. He drew them to services and converted them. Many of them, he bewailed, returned to evil ways without options (*Against,* 56f). He worked with other clergy to get Jimmy Walker elected Mayor of New York, which changed the attitude of the Police Vice squad from passive to active cooperation. That a prostitute taught her daughter the evil work saddened him, as the girl died of syphilis at fourteen years of age (57f). He preached against sexual immorality among Harlem elites; stirred up such animosity that a prominent Psychologist sent him a death threat, with twenty–nine others (71). Such sermons as "Little Foxes" and "Watch Your Step" exhorted renunciation of sexual and related evils. He favored moral ways and enterprises. His courteous, considerate, gentle manner of relating to people made his Puritan morality hard to resist. His rebellious son wrote that his father's Puritanism was sharpened by his gentleness (*Adam,* 29). The meek method was inductive and natural for him. Not always effective, as he felt indifference was the most numbing of foes (*Against,* 75). Moral economics was a major concern. In the conduct of Immanuel and Abyssinian finances, great pains were taken to ensure the moral integrity of the people entrusted with financial management (171ff). Self–control of money was power; dependence on someone else's money was another form of slavery. He opposed all forms of dependence on European–Americans.

Another moral crusade was Powell's assault on wasting money that should help others. His crusade did not parrot; it liberated. He criticized ostentatious funeral spending (84f). His opposition to extravagance was famous. The main African sins were extravagance, eating, drinking, sleeping, frolicking, talking, showing off and burying too much money in cemeteries (173). He crusaded against selfishness in favor of giving. The relationship between giving and receiving was a mystery, as Jesus stated in Luke 6.38; he said the world may not be old enough yet to know it (155). Luke 9.24 did not mean to stop reading and studying and become imbeciles, empty sapheads, mental nobodies; fail to behave morally and become loose enough to be morally bankrupt (167f). The life of the mind and heart leads to moral standards of extravagant generosity.

Equality was a hermeneutical principle for Powell. Beyond the individual self, the principle he acted upon in all relationships was equality between women and men in marriage and work, of the races in education, housing, employment, economics and politics. He spelled this out in numerous sermons and articles, including a June, 1930 article in *Home and Foreign Mission Fields*, the Missionary Journal of the Southern Baptist Convention (180). He opposed homosexual people ambivalently. He found the basis for sexual equality in Genesis 3 and the usual rejection of homosexuals in Genesis 19 (215f), but reported guest ministers in his pulpit arrested for homosexuality, because it was illegal. He knew congregations that called homosexual pastors on their release from prison. His Puritanism imposed limits on deepening emotions of sympathy and love as ethical progress. Until his private papers will be open to scholars, we cannot answer some questions. For example, was he aware that Countee Cullen, the famous Harlem Renaissance Poet and adopted son of a Methodist Pastor who was his close friend, was a closeted homosexual man?

Racism was the moral cause, however, that he took up most often and with the greatest passion ("Mencken," and 247–255). Amid streets running with bloody riots, he read newspaper reports and heard radio broadcasts of lynch in and burning of African–American towns and neighborhoods across the nation. Still, meekness was the method by which African–Americans conquered enemies (270ff). He included agitation and marches as expressions of meekness.

On the other side of the Atlantic, unbeknown to Powell, Max Scheler described an ontological phenomenology of the world come of age similar to Kidd's and Powell's. The world come of age featured the re-sublimation of human powers of reason. Half–Jewish, convert to and out of Catholicism, he believed Western civilization was in for a revolution of drives, from those associated with reason to those associated with emotion. Children over adults, women over men, the masses over the elites, the colored peoples over the white, psychology, the unconscious reality, over culture and society, the conscious reality. The ancient emphasis on the intellectual, ascetic, Homeric philosophy gave way to the emotional, hedonistic, Dionysian philosophy. The rebellion was an organic necessity (Manfred Frings, *Max Scheler, A Concise Introduction into the World of a Great Thinker,* 199). He created a phenomenological ontology consisting of anthropology and ethics, like colleague Husserl, both unlike Heidegger, Husserl's student, whose phenomenology is ontological but without anthropology and ethics. Johann Gottfried von

Herder, another Sociologist, agreed with Scheler and Husserl: There is no person without community and no community without the Spirit as the act–center of the individual and the community (Frings, 204). Hitler suppressed their works; Heidegger escorted his doctoral mentor, Husserl, a Jew, out of Frieburg University library on orders from Hitler, and was the philosophical apologist for National Socialism. The phenomenology of Scheler and Husserl, but also Heidegger, inspired form–critical studies and interpretations of the Bible, as K. Barth stated (*Church Dogmatics,* Part I, Volume 2, n., 728). Without the spectacles of a world–view or ontological phenomenology, whether of Wilhelm Dilthey, Scheler and Husserl, Kierkegaard's objection to Hegel was stillborn in the Teutonic religious, cultural and social context. Scheler's part in tradition–historical and form–critical hermeneutics took the form of rebellion against individualistic and aristocratic–elitist interpretation, while Heidegger in–spired such studies as Bultmann's, which deleted miracles and altruism in favor of the raw motives of power and conquest. Charles H. Dodd combined individual with corporate hermeneutics, on the Anglo–Saxon side (Markus Barth, *Conversation with the Bible,* 130ff). One result of form–critical hermeneutics, following Husserl and Scheler, emphasized that the Bible contained sermons, school lessons, Confessions of faith, prayers, poetry, and songs which exhorted people to responsive action (300). The use of this method in Powell and European and European–American interpreters joyfully and freely discovered inherent energies, cultural and social realities and distinctive literary forms. Again, the Bible was a charter of freedom coinciding with the larger, inevitable, phenomenological revolution occurring in Western civilization. As a result of deepening emotion according to the Spirit of Jesus, meekness was the powerful force that effected desirable personal, social, cultural, religious and global change. Meekness was costly obedience, not cheap grace. Challenging and converting violent and wanton people in the world come of age, not adapting the Gospel to them, as the church did so many times, the correlation of Biblical energies with emotions was a comfortable fit between Biblical theology and secular philosophy. The crux of this connection was what Scheler called the *ordo amoris,* the downward turn of love. Jose Gassett y Ortega was the leading Spanish Existential, socialist philosopher whose work Bonhoeffer read in prison. He stressed the same point, but were Bonhoeffer's heart and mind opened to comprehend this theme all the more because of his six months immersed in a deliberate, well–thought–out program of ethical progress through emotionalization based on Spiritual Biblical interpretation combined with Kidd's *Science of Power* with his exaltation of Christ–like love as our one hope for peace and justice?

The problem was that when Dilthey imported hermeneutics, the science of interpretation, from its natural home in theology, compassion barely hung on. By the time Heidegger took over hermeneutics, compassion disappeared completely. Scheler, Husserl, Martin Buber, Karl Jaspers, Jacques Maritain and others saw this more clearly than the young Bonhoeffer, who went around Union explaining Heidegger's project in an appreciative way. Powell knew from Kidd's *Science* that success in compassion and love required a vital, powerful, emotional, truthful force to which persons were drawn and freely yielded, abandoning destructive behaviors in exchange for new patterns of behavior. The sympathy and love of Jesus Christ comprised the deepened psychological truth necessary to create this vital program of reformation for religion, anthropology, sociology and psychology. Maybe, as Scheler, Husserl, Buber, Jaspers, Maritain, K. Barth and Dodd proposed, this was possible through an ontological phenomenology of the inherent spiritual and compassionate nature of people; Biblical interpretation was as impossible without philosophy, said K. Barth, as humanity was impossible without sin (Op Cit, 728f). For Powell, the struggle of his "flies in the buttermilk" to break free of oppression was a life–or–death choice, the philosophy that enabled him to read the Bible in the first place. If the Bible was only comprehensible through the eyeglasses of philosophy, as K. Barth maintained, why not the philosophy of universal love, freedom, justice, peace and joy? Why not ethical progress through the deepening of the emotions of sympathy and love women lead? Why not the social–ethical phenomenology of Scheler, Husserl, Jaspers, Gabriel Marcel or Molefi Asante? Open up the conversation, HOMILIA, Greek for conversation used in the word homiletics and not commit what Barth calls the grotesque comedy of those insisting there is only way of interpreting the Bible.

Oh, yes, one more word: The old Anglo–Saxon folk song, "Skip to My Lou My Darling," contains the words, "Flies in the buttermilk, shoo fly, shoo!" White folk are the "buttermilk," and colored folk are the "flies." Powell's people were the "flies" the "buttermilk" folk shooed away. That was and is the ugly, broad ditch forming the frontier for ethical progress, which we must emotionalize people to make, humbling ourselves under divine love; otherwise, we never cross the boundary.

Chapter Four

Progress Through the Love of Jesus

Giovanni Papini, 1881–1956, is less obscure today than Kidd or Harris, with two Websites on the Internet. Much discussion today concerns his role in creating the political philosophy of Futurism, which was part of Benito Mussolini's Fascist program that he supported, even after he abandoned Futurism. He received the Mussolini Prize for Literature during Fascism, which was not a factor in Powell's appropriation of his biography of Jesus. Powell appropriated something from him, since his biography of Jesus was one of the books Ferris noted that Powell read. He started writing at fourteen. A sixty–fifth book was published posthumously–*Happiness of the Unhappy*–he died July 8, 1956. He suffered from a debilitating disease. Limbs and eyes useless, he dictated books and newspaper articles to his granddaughter, one letter of the alphabet at a time (C. Maranza, "Papini: Warrior at Rest," *The Catholic World*, October, 1957, 45–49. *Happiness* was not published in the U. S.) A brilliant, passionate, creative force even as life ebbed away. From a raging, fiery anarchist and atheist, Papini became an ardent Catholic. First World War experiences led to his conversion and book, *The Life of Christ* (1927). The book Powell read was his biggest international best–seller. Samuel Putnam wrote that he imagined himself a saint, hero, a reforming demiurge who destroyed, created, and inspired people (in "A Letter from Italy," *Saturday Review of Literature*, Feb. 15, 1930, 739.) His father, an atheist, kept all religious influences from him. His discovery of Jesus resulted from disgust and disgruntlement with the Futurism he invented and all other philosophies and religions (from Mazza, 189–195). An anarchist who shot off pistols in movie theaters and other acts of terror disrupting complacent Italian society was his hooligan way of life before his conversion to the religion of Jesus. Not even then, however, did he agree with his mentor, Benedetto Croce, in whose works intuition and feeling, rather than abstract reason, were the source of the truth functioning through conflicting forces as thought by Hegel. Croce opposed the Fascism Papini embraced. The question at the end of the Hegelian dialectic, the form the synthesis would take, remained open for Croce but not for Papini.

Since Ferris did not refer to any other works of Papini except *Life*, I examined that book alone. The work was important for Papini since all subsequent works carried the same essential message, "the salvation of society through the universal application of the Law of Love." (191.) The destruction and suffering during the latter part of World War I deeply depressed him. He turned for help to the novels of Leo Tolstoy and Fyodor Dostoyevsky. Their Spirituality impelled him to read the Gospels again. He read them several times before with a hostile and diffident attitude, but the War experience transformed him so that he read the Sermon on the Mount with insights from the Russian novelists thinking only of saving people from repeating the terrors of war. Suddenly, life was worth loving whether or not it meant anything, a truth that comforted him in his suffering and physical degeneration. He meditated on the Gospels. The only safeguard against terrorism, he decided, is a radical change in people's souls. He felt people must leave savagery and hatred behind in exchange for the holiness and love for enemies found in Christianity, which remedied humanity's ills. He wrote *Storia di Cristo* in the solitude of his farm, away from his native Florence. He went there not for the usual solitude and tranquility, nor to write a book for financial success, but because of an inner restlessness that impelled him to write something that would help another person. After writing the book, he was driven to belong to a Christ–founded society and found his spiritual home with a Franciscan congregation in Florence. (191f.) A proclivity borne of suffering and terror similar to the African–American experience in the United States changed his attitude toward the Gospels the hunger and thirst and emptiness of which, initiated transformation, energizing his prodigious skills as an author and whetting his appetite for more, through the community modeled on the basis of Francis of Assisi, servant of the poor and all living things.

Powell, Indianapolis, 1909, said we cannot be Christians without Christ's love and if we love Jesus we will join his church (*Against*, 64). The First World War motivated him to write *Patriotism and the Negro* in which he took a pacifist stance based on Jesus' teaching, but in which he also used the military experience of African–Americans to leverage cultural, social and economic elevation for the masses. In 1924, he re–

called an encounter in Berlin with an elderly woman on The Avenue of Victory, with rows of statues glorifying war. An army company goose-stepped by and she remarked to him that they were nothing to be proud of. He celebrated her attitude as the one necessary to drive the war demons from earth (93).

World War I was a crisis for people of most nations. Kidd responded toward the end of his life in 1916 to the same need as Papini. At the end of the Second World War, in 1946, Papini published *The Letters of Pope Celestine VI to All Mankind* (1948), a mythic pope, emphasizing the same themes as his *Storia*. Mazza saw him not as apologist, philosopher or logician, but as a "poet of ideas." She felt that he was energetic, spent thirty years frantic, looking for God and, finding God, was a most zealous disciple, wielding his pen to compel everyone to prostrate themselves at Jesus' feet, to love and serve Him (Mazza, 193, 195). Powell could identify with that history. His hoodlum years preceded his conversion, after which he was a most zealous disciple and lover of Jesus. Remember the message that Bonhoeffer repeated hearing at Abyssinian Church? However evil we may be, Jesus the Christ had the power to save us (*Against,* 62). Papini's transformation from Anarchist-terrorist to a humble, joyful Franciscan Christian was like one transformed from an immoral hoodlum to a humble, joyful, Progressive Christian–Powell himself.

Papini's sweeping criticisms in the beginning of his *Storia* appealed to a lot of Powell's criticisms. Papini felt that Jesus scholars of his day mistook their libraries for barns, caricaturing them as presumptuous Mules, drunk with metaphysics and philology. Jesus became a legend with a natural life, part prophet, part necromancer, part demagogue hypnotizing disciples, not dying but regaining consciousness in the tomb and then duping people into thinking he is raised from death (*Storia*, 1). He objected to Jesus critics who claimed he was a myth, the Gospels only jumbles of gesticulations. He disliked those who thought Jesus a good fellow, if a bit pretentious, who studied in a Hellenistic academy and Buddhism and belonged to the Essenes, guilty of plagiarism. He disdained those who thought Jesus a prescient Liberal humanitarian or Rousseau democrat. Neither did Jesus belong under psychiatric care (1f).

Powell criticized Jesus scholars of his day in homiletic form. All the African atheists, agnostics and humanists in America would not even fill the main floor of a great hall, for they did not rationalize away the truth of God, the Bible, Jesus and religion, but accepted all on the basis of faith (*Against*, 275). There were atheist and agnostic ex-slaves whose indifference and immorality bothered him (Raboteau).

Papini critically engaged all philosophical and religious choices of which he was aware in *Storia* and in his literary magazines and newspaper columns. He criticized worshipers of Truth, Spirit, Proletariat, Hero, Humanity, Rationalism, Imperialism, Reason, Beauty, Peace, Sorrow, Pity, Ego, the Future and so on (*Storia*, 2). He made room for Jesus. He objected to those who dethroned Christianity or God by removing their spine. Dismissing mystics, he disliked political and philosophical writers. Infallibilists were objects of harsh attacks. Infallible substitutes for Jesus included Freemasons, Spiritualists, Theosophists, Occultists and Scientists. He especially hated Nietzsche, referring to his death of venereal disease in Italy with relish. This agreed with Powell's bias against Mencken. Nietzsche's follower wrote many editorials in his magazines and books defending him, including agreeing with his desultory opinion of women. Many people despised Jesus in Papini's time. Cusswords were involuntary attestations to the presence of Jesus (3). Powell supported the African–American Masonic Lodge and did not think they are out to displace Jesus. Among the segments of Soteriology was a call for all people to rehearse Jesus' tender, heart-breaking emotional weeping over the sins of Jerusalem (*Against*, 281). Weeping over sins (Luke 19.41), driving currency exchangers out of the temple (John 2.15), cursing the barren fig tree (Mark 14.71), weeping when he heard Lazarus died (John 11.35), compassionate because people were like shepherdless sheep (Mark 6.34), sensitive enough to feel a woman's touch amid a crowd of people (Mark 5.30); everywhere in the gospels Jesus was full of emotions.

Papini concerned the many who felt furious toward Jesus; they proved Jesus lives. The duty of every generation was to write a Gospel based on their context. He set aside questions of philological glosses, exegetical commentaries, erudite scholars, emendations they made to the Biblical text, as he aimed his work at the human heart, the emotional center (*Storia*, 4). He decried saccharine, maudlin, pietistic biographies of Jesus; his aim was to translate the Gospels to help lost people, those as bewildered as him (5). His natural passion dominated his writing of his generation's Gospel. He was, in Powell's words, working because of a sense of God's power rising within him (*Palestine*, 151). The critical question with which he interrogated Papini was how successfully he brought Jesus' Spirit into this world (217).

Papini started out well enough on the zeal of Tolstoy and Dostoyevsky and his reaction to the terrors of war, took hold of the Gospels with the tenacity of a hungry dog biting a bone. He presented Jesus' story as unusually as possible. Violent contrasts and foreshortenings, crude, vividly emotional words startle apathetic, jaded, modern souls used to highly colored errors. He made them see the truth whether they wanted to or not (Op cit, 5ff). The Hebrew context and Greek antiquity were the background against which he depicted Jesus as greater than all who came before him (11). The self-educated writer used words to create an ardent expression of faith in Jesus (12ff). He created a book-length sermon over and against the mediocre homilies of Catholic priests, aiming his Jesus sermon at people who never heard sermons (15). Jesus was the central hermeneutical truth, force and power of both men. Powell built Abyssinian Church for twenty-nine years, working day and night, to sickness and nervous breakdowns, obviously not to build himself up, but centering his life and the lives of others on Jesus, his rock and redeemer. He did not want the gates of hell to stand a chance at destroying what he built (*Against*, 287, interpreting Matthew 7.24f). He had a "Highways and Hedges Society," for example, interpreting Matthew 22.1-14 and Luke 14.16-24, to bring waifs and street people to Abyssinian's Soup Kitchen, emergency housing and educational and job referral programs. Similarly, Papini found most religions, churches and other options repulsive in relation to Jesus (Op cit, 16f). Powell worked as a Pastor-theologian who wrote; Papini as a writer-theologian who preached. Both aimed to provoke an apathetic, bored, jaded, supposedly sophisticated people of a world come of age (*Against*, 141).

Papini's interpretation of Jesus was part of an intense conversion after the horrors of war and thirty years of searching, not a discrete piece of diffident or indifferent scholarship. Some academic treatments of Jesus in his day lacked vitality, not critically engaging real events. He attacked such authors because of their apparent lack of provocative experience and lack of concern for provocative presentation, which fit in with Harris's and Powell's notion of experience as the ground of religion.

Powell believed Jesus was wounded for his sins, cleansed him from all evil, and transformed him into a new creature (*Palestine*, 151). Jesus taught him to find life by losing himself in service to others. He agreed with Jesus' purpose, to meet the social and spiritual needs of people (*Against*, 167 and "Social," 15). He committed to make Jesus real in the world and in the U. S. (*Upon This Rock*, 117). Jesus prayed for unity through loving each other; so he understood Jesus' Priestly Prayer, John 17.23 (*Against*, 192f). Jesus disallowed hunger, said as much about supplying needs of body as about soul needs. His first preachers he commanded to feed the people. Organizing a "Relief Bureau" in Jerusalem was spiritual (Acts 4.23-35, 221). Jesus espoused Spiritual meekness and the policy of non- resistance in the Sermon on the Mount which also impressed Papini. Powell called Jesus' Beatitudes a philosophy of meekness (271). Nevertheless, Jesus was no philosopher, no dogmatist in the academic sense and no maker of creeds, but exemplified perfect human being. Unlike Moses and Elijah, Jesus ideally served and loved others (*Palestine,* 99, 152ff).

Powell attended a seminar at Yale in 1931 entitled, "The Task of the Church." Both African and European clergy participated. The seminar found that Capitalism fundamentally opposed Jesus' teachings, contrary to the well-being of workers. The seminar assigned role of taking a stand for social righteousness to the African church. They called on that church to develop sharper prophetic proclamations and new, fearless techniques to apply the faith of Jesus to transform society. The type of leadership Gandhi provided for India the seminar wanted Africans to do for the US and was what Jesus did for the world (Welty, 289f). The power of meekness was brought home to him in a new way, as he heard for one of the first times in his career an open, free acknowledgement of the uniqueness of the African Church from European professors and clergy. His appreciation of Gandhi found support and his commitment to non-violent struggling for justice and freedom. Evidently, there was no such expectation of European clergy, which was another reason why St. Peter's or Trinity Lutheran, Riverside Church and Broadway Presbyterian failed to meet Bonhoeffer's Spiritual needs. Shamefully, Yale Divinity had no record of the seminar and Union had no record of Powell's sermons in their chapel.

Papini went along with Mussolini's political program. Powell did not. Hitler, Stalin and Mussolini exemplified how close the world was to the second coming of Jesus, they were so evil (*Against,* 141). Papini asserted, however, the re-establishing of Israel in Palestine was all that the world lacked to prepare for Christ's second coming (*Storia,* 274). His Tuscan pride was as unmistakable as his low opinion of women and anti-Semitism. In these regards, he limited, truncated and rendered Jesus impotent. In the final analysis, the freedom of Jesus was the standard gauging all hermeneutics. The rise of existence philosophy, or existentialism, occurred in the same historical epoch as Powell's ministry. The value of emotion and intuition over reason was one of the truths or dogmas of existentialists from Jean-Paul Sartre and K. Marx on one side to Heidegger and Hitler on the other. On one side, people asserted values and make moral decisions from Nothingness while on the other, Nothingness was morality. Existentialism was the basis for theologians like K. Barth, R. Niebuhr, P. Tillich, R. Bultmann and, very differently, A. Cochrane (*The Existentialists and God*).The extent to which K. Barth's existentialism was like Sartre's was Eberhard Juengel's finding. The freedom of human subjects to feel God the Other living subject was a theme in Barth's work and the existential theologians who marched for civil rights with the insignificant others their cultures and societies oppressed. The basic emotions, joy, anger, fear and sadness, evoked a theological turn in some philosophers.

Papini and Powell started faith journeys in the midst of suffering, terror, war and disillusionment. They discovered the power of suffering, redeeming love in Jesus and both aimed at the heart, the emotions of people. They suffered indignities because of aspects of their bodies over which they had no control–Powell's race and Papini's disease. Both abandoned Pacifist positions as the Second World War took shape, the terms of engagement powerfully transformed their emotions. Powell emotionally changed for the ideal of democracy while Papini emotionally changed for the ideal of Roman, Tuscan supremacy. Powell's struggle, however, assaulted his own nation as well as the Axis powers, for his enemy was racism, a spiritual disease afflicting the U. S. and Europe. While suffering was a hermeneutic principle they shared in common, the result of their beginning in divine suffering diverged very sharply. Powell's support was not for the U.S., however, but for the United Nations and, at that level, for peace.

The terrible weight of Jesus' baptismal burden staggered Jesus' humanity in John 17, a centerpiece of Powell's Christ–centered theology. His sermon based on John 17 followed his return to the Pulpit from a nervous breakdown after years of work around the clock to feed, educate, house and employ Harlem Africans the Great Depression impoverished. That December Sunday, with Bonhoeffer in attendance, he asserted that Jesus was wounded for the sins of the world, including ours. In Jesus God hungered, like us (*Palestine,* 97).

Moreover, both shared a common goal, to reform the church and society according to the principle of the universal love of Jesus. Powell's limiting ambivalence led him to disregard homosexuals while Papini's limiting Tuscan Pride made him support Mussolini and have a low opinion of women and Jews. Nevertheless, Papini's book, *The Devil* (1953), recapitulated Origen's finding that even the Satan can be saved through the love of Jesus (Read reviews of *The Devil* in *Time,* January 4, 1954 and *Newsweek,* November 4, 1954, 84). Powell's motto in the face of hostility is: The one who loves is superior to the one who hates (*Riots,* 110 and "Enrichment," 843).

Papini and Powell lived rough lives before conversion. They applied the love of Jesus to other hoodlums. Papini preached through writing,

Powell, in orations newspapers and magazines published. About the rioters in Harlem during the Second World War, he called on the powers that were not to shoot or send rioters to Reform School, but to make them brothers because he was proof that hoodlums can change (*Riots,* 62). Whether they change or not, were their lives worthwhile although they did not mean the same as other lives? This question remained at the end of Hegel's historical dialectic and drove Kierkegaard's philosophy of the subject and much of existential philosophy; for example, Jacques Derrida's revolt against the institutionalization of the insane. Powell took street–corner hoodlums in tow to run his public gym in the community center, for example.

Papini had a provocative homiletic principle, to startle and shock bored moderns out of sloth and apathy. He provoked their hearts to show them a new, fresh, vital Jesus. The heart, the center of emotion was where we must provoke distraught people for the faith of Jesus to emerge from within and transform them. Powell shared provocative, shocking rhetoric as a hermeneutic principle with him. By 1902, in his lecture and article about Douglass he paraphrased Jesus' parable of the Good Samaritan, Luke 10.29–37, to work in a way he felt would shock people as much as Jesus' original shocking oratory. Jesus and Douglass hurled powerful anathemas, or curses, against religious machines. Their withering, fiery sarcasm piled deep on the heads of religious leaders. The pious fled from the wounded man by the roadside, Jesus and Douglass. ("Douglass," 340.) He struggled to overcome indifference but felt his efforts were all in vain. Both men aimed to shock people out of indifference. The Holy Spirit of Jesus Christ was the enemy of apathy.

Papini also defended Jesus in the face of his critics. Classical Roman Catholic homiletic theory after Augustine was within the framework of Aristotle–Cicero forensic rhetoric. As a defense attorney proved the innocence of his client in the face of accusations by the pro–secutor, the preacher functioned in the court of public opinion to defend Jesus against his critics (Joseph Connors wrote about forensic rhetoric in *Catholic Homiletic Theory in Historical Perspective,* 1962). Papini conformed. Forensic hermeneutics afflicted Fundamentalism, but not Powell. Marcus Barth provided another criticism of Fundamentalism's use of legalistic rhetoric many years after Papini and Powell (*Conversation,* 110–114, 117, 120, 127, 153ff, 187, 240 and 254).

Papini thought the only choice was Dante's, a fellow Florentine Tuscan, between nothingness and God (Op cit, 18). Powell said to be without God meant no hope, no joy, no friend during troubles, no partner in death's dark vale (*Palestine,* 113f). No one, with the possible excep-

exceptions of the rich young ruler who was too rich to follow Jesus on his own terms (Matthew 19.22) and his opponents (Matthew 26.4) and betrayer (Mark 14.10–18) of Jesus, everyone who came to Jesus went away feeling good, not bad (Ibid, 184). Matthew depicted a people without Jesus in a region of darkness under death's dark shadow (*Palestine,* 113, regarding Matthew 4.16, 6.23, 8.12, 22.13, 25.30 and 27.45).

Born in a dirty barn, wrote Papini, Jesus had nothing to do with ornate Italian crèches (Op cit, 21). The poverty of God in Jesus' life and death stood in sharp contrast to Western wealth, which led him to romanticize peasants, carpenters, masons and shepherds as more naturally honest than wealthy people (22n 35f, for examples). He was not optimistic, however, about elevating the masses (59), a point at which Powell diverged from him. He essayed the history of donkeys as deities (Ibid, 22), the Zoroastrian faith of the Magi in Matthew 2 (24f). His anti–Semitism stuck out like a snake when he called Herod a "half–civilized Arab." (28, 350.) He thought money and the Bible were the means by which Jews dominated the world (Ibid, 46, also Leonard Bacon's "Wild Man's Lexicon," in *Saturday Review of Literature*, 3f). He grudgingly cited three Jewish achievements. They conceived of God as one universal parent. Rich, their God favored the poor and negated riches. They loved enemies (Op cit, 45). He traced Jesus back to Jewish prophets; His destiny found direction in prophetic laments, full of fire (49). He used the word "liberator" to describe Jesus (57), displacing John the Baptizer, who was an accuser, not a liberator. He told the liberating love of Jesus in the midst of modern Christianity for transformational purposes. In Jesus was no feverish, obstinate, proselytizer trying to work off guilt because of some past sin. Jesus' love was natural, not dutiful, fraternal, spontaneous and friendly with no reproach, no effort to overcome repugnance. Jesus found purity in the impure that have no fear of getting dirty, knew he cleansed through the love felt by the Saints, such lofty love as made all other loves vulgar (60). Jesus transformed the world's kingdoms into God's kingdom (66). No elitist, setting himself up over people, Jesus went among them (67). The social revolution of the loving Jesus transformed the human spirit so that despotic religion, culture and society were forgotten. No more King–subject, master–slave, rich–poor, self–righteous against humble righteous and no more free–prisoner divisions (74). Conversion was the revolution of all of life, all the values, feelings, opinions and intentions, as Jesus put the matter in Matthew 5–7, which he found in the works of Rousseau, Progressives, Evolutionists, Monists, Marxists, Mathematic philosophers (like Bertrand Russell), Protestants and French revolutionaries, in that they were all over–turners. Jesus, for Papini, was the supreme, fearless, radical maker of paradoxes, the eternal overturner (94). If Jesus erred, the Nihilists, like Heidegger, were right, said he and we must all believe in nothing (97). Self–preservation opposed the love of Jesus in his program. Love of enemies was the acid test of conversion. Hate yourself and love your enemy, which just started as well as tested the final result of conversion to the faith of Jesus and the only way to have no enemies on earth (111).

Papini limited Asian religious concepts of love to respect and indulgence or to prudence and mildness, short of love of enemies (112f). The Egyptian religion of Osiris limited peace to decimating warfare (114). While Zarathustra left Persia the law agreeing with Isaiah 61 and Luke 4, he left nothing about loving enemies (115). Buddha loved wretched and despised people, through Nirvana but Buddha's love, self–seeking and chilly, egoistic, was indifferent, stoic in grief and joy and did not love enemies (114).

Papini used love of enemies as a principle for interpretation, however brief and partial. Critically, he evaluated the evolution of the Biblical concept of enemy relationships from Exodus 21.34 to Matthew 5.38–42 and Luke 6.29f. He found no such teaching anywhere among the Greeks and Romans (115–122). There was no egalitarian feeling in his view of women as slaves of their bodies, slaves of weakness and the desires of males. Thus drawn to Jesus, he said she loved him and asked for water (John 4.7–28), silent attention (Luke 10.39, 42) and such (Ibid, 220), far from Powell's recounting of the saying that women were the last of Jesus' disciples at the cross and the first at His tomb (*Palestine,* 179).

Papini saw in Jesus' death on the cross a judgment of society and the church a lot like Powell. After the First World War, people sorrowed, politicians and princes betrayed them, power elites deceived them, oppressive royals killed them, the rich made them weep, priests and preachers thought more about their bellies than of their Lord (Op cit, 347f). The eternal Jesus, here, now, invisible, benevolent, wanted life in the present moments now to anticipate heaven on earth (Ibid, 408). In miracles, Jesus impressed him. Jesus reluctantly healed people and never claimed credit, interpreting His miracles as rewards of the faith of those receiving his blessing, such as Matthew 8.10–13, 9.2–22, 29, 15.28, 21.21ff (131). Jesus was neither ascetic nor ostentatious in his renunciation of wealth (Matthew 6.24, 13.22, Mark 10.23) unlike other religious and philosophical leaders. Material poverty, like humility, was part of the process of grace perfecting nature, of the journey through sanctification to justifying, perfect faith, following the juxtaposing of sanctification and justification by Thomas Aquinas in *Summa* (200). He interpreted Luke 16.19–31, Jesus' Parable of the Rich Man and Lazarus. Powell differed from him concerning the parable. In 1915, he said Jesus never wanted people with money to go to hell, nor for every poor beggar to go to heaven. He was glad there was only one Parable like this in the New Testament because every time an African had two cents to rub together some preacher used Luke 16.19–31 to condemn her or him. He favored Labor Unions and other economic, organized structures to share wealth fairly. The Parable of Lazarus was about paying attention of Mosaic legislation and Jesus about the responsible use of wealth, as in the Parable of the Dishonest Steward in Luke 16.8–11 (Welty, 22). Voluntary poverty caused rich people to strip themselves for the love of Jesus; of his own upper middle class, he felt that they do so little for the poor they had no right to condemn them (Op cit, 201). His hypothesis was that if the middle class loved people more, they became better people (200).

In the wake of the First World War and although his protagonists painted him as a former anarchist, evidently overlooking his appreciation for fellow Anarchists, Godwin, Stirner, Proudhon and Kropotkin, in applying Matthew 22.15–22, Mark 12.13–17 and Luke 20.20–26. He joined the assault on manipulating peace to justify war, make Jesus support Genghis Khan or Napoleon Bonaparte, refine extreme Islamic terrorism. All perpetrated the Gospel text they all knew but failed to understand (206). He favored Jesus–based criticism of Capitalism, like Ambrose of Milan and Dante of Florence before him (250f). Jesus gave eternal life, interpreted the Parable of the Final Judgment (Matthew 25.31–46), to the nation that gives even a little life to poor folk (265). The problem of Jesus' teaching on poverty, suffering, charity and wealth was more complex for Powell than for him. They agreed that faith was the real crisis we face in war terrors (*Palestine,* 194) and on the total nature of conversion ("Model"). Nevertheless, Pascal's famous Wager was interpreted one way by Papini, embracing the totality of Roman Catholicism and another way by Powell, embracing the Gospel of Jesus in the four gospels of the New Testament but not the doctrines and creeds of the church (Op cit, 151). Hebrew atoms danced four thousand years, Powell said, producing Jesus, who influenced, but did not control, art, social service, government and literature (*Riots,* 99f). Considering that Douglass influenced Powell to interpret the Bible as a charter of freedom as the Spirituals revealed God's freeing nature and his allegiance to the New England Spiritual hermeneutics of King and

Harris, setting their philosophy strongly against Fundamentalism and Liberalism and his use of Kidd's post–war philosophy of power free from social Darwinism and given his reading of Papini, how else could he respond to attacks, criticisms and death threats for his efforts to feed hungry people than not be able to understand how fellow clergy possibly opposed him (*Upon This Rock,* 16f). His egalitarian work with women and Jews opposed Papini. He celebrated Jewish survival of holocausts of persecution for 4,000 years (*Riots,* 99). He wanted African–Americans to celebrate January First as Emancipation Proclamation Day as Jews celebrate Passover, the day of their liberation (33), but European–Americans did not allow it, which changed in the 1960s with the invention of Kwanza by African–Americans. Moreover, Powell thought charity is a poor substitute for justice, like Harris. Concerning European–American support of African–American colleges, he thinks it bad for the donors and worse for the receivers. He knew every human race had faults (*Against,* 181). On close examination, so did Papini, although his pride and racism were unmistakable. Just because someone recognized Jesus is the most gentle, meek, non–violent revolutionary, a radical overturner of class systems did not mean the same results. The philosophical principles connecting the exegesis to reality this present moment now dimmed or diffused the Gospel as much as sin. Both were eschatological, passionate, evangelistic and socially, politically transforming, but one was an anarchist who chose radical Right, Fascist politics while the other was a democratic socialist choosing the moderate but racially inclusive, radical Left.

Max Scheler, a contemporary of Papini and Powell, passed by them like a ship in the night. The son of a Jewish mother and German Protestant father, he was concerned about religion subverting emotions. Manfred Frings noted of his viewpoint that he found both philosophers of power, Plato and Aristotle, incompatible with the love of Jesus. The Greek idea of love, above all, lacked any downward direction. The direction of love, whether EROS, AGAPE or PHILIOS in their philosophies moves up toward elitism, as both taught elite power-brokers, Plato served as official philosopher to Philip of Macedonia and Aristotle served his son, Alexander the Great. The downward turn of love, the *ordo amoris,* made the love of Jesus unique (Frings, 170).

Papini, Kidd and Powell criticized Capitalism more than Harris. Powell used the word materialism. For them, Jesus challenged the oppressiveness of Capitalism. Later, Helmut Gollwitzer wrote that whether Rome, Geneva or Wittenberg theology, whether justification comes before or after good works, whether the winner was the Puritan

Oliver Cromwell or the Catholic Charles I, for the red, yellow and black folk of planet Earth the result was the same, domination by the Capitalist revolution (quoted by Allan Boesak in *Farewell to Innocence*, 31). No matter how you slice it, before Boesak or Gollwitzer, much less Papini and Powell, Western Imperialism during the 18th century and following was truculent, greedy and cynical. (J.H. Parry, *The Establishment of the European Hegemony, 1415–1715,* 192.)

In a similar vein, K. Barth felt that when interest–bearing capital displaces humanity, the increase of capital became the object comprising the goal and meaning of the political conversation, the means set in motion that required men to kill and be killed (*Church Dogmatics,* Part III, Volume 4, 459). This was why Powell saw the world turn from Capitalism to the economics of Jesus Christ (*Riots,* 109). The turning inspired him to think equally meaningful and salaried work a real possibility for Africans in the U. S. and Africa. A Christ–transformed society directed the power of money to liberation instead of perdition. (Also K. Barth, Op cit, 531f.)

The social problem of human equality was given to Papini, Powell, Kidd, Harris and the rest, including Scheler and Heidegger, Barth and Gollwitzer, as well as Tillich and Macquarrie. The problem materialism presented was thinking and treating other people as means to an end. People were objects. Was not this act inherently unequal, inequitable and selfish? (543.) Did we witness at all the rise and fall of empires driven by a ruling, profiteering mandate that even made Marxism a form of unequal objectification? (544.) Powell asserted progress through the love of Jesus for women and men, poor and rich and the forms of social progress toward equalization available to him between 1870 and 1920, responding to the First World War, he revised formats, kept his influence going in both the Bookerite and DuBois camps between 1930 and his demise in 1953. Capitalism was never any be–all or end–all of his program; emotionalization of the ideal of the universal love of Jesus was the standard under which he subsumed any and every other power beginning with himself (by the way, 545). This was his economics. There was, in Jesus Christ, an ongoing, eternal, liberating revolution of God against all ungodliness and unrighteousness, all that did not agree with the meek, loving creation of total equality ended, while only that which agreed with God's revolution continued.

Chapter Five

Toward a Progressive Church

Powell reformed the church. Making the church progress was a principle of interpretation. He took Progressive critics of religion seriously; lectures and articles on Abolitionists set the tone for his career, not just anarchists, but active revolutionaries, both violent and non–violent. Progressive faith did not wait with folded arms for God to act. What was the duty of Progressive Reformation? To assist God's providence, strenuously working for the God who helped those who help themselves. ("Douglass," 341.) Gayraud Wilmore noted that from George Liele and David George to Cone and himself, African theology was an apologetics for the just and righteous God, often by implication and indirectly, in fact a criticism of the apostasy of European–American churches (Wilmore, "Black Christians, Church Unity and One Common Expression of Apostolic Faith," in *Black Witness*, 12 for more on Liele and George, Raboteau, 139ff.) In other words, Africans reformed European–American churches, not always directly, explicitly and progressively like Powell. Was this the next reformation of which Bonhoeffer wrote after 1931? Powell explicitly, directly and progressively opposed the cheap grace of apostate European–American churches in 1908, when Bonhoeffer was two years old ("Douglass," 340). Just as explicitly and directly he reformed African–American churches under Progressive discipleship (343). If Abolitionist critics were infidel, as Fundamentalist interpreters maintained, then Jesus was infidel, too (339f). The true church differed from the false, slave–owning church. He felt Douglass a Christian in spite of the Church. (340.) He shared Douglass's commitment to revolutionary, rebellious freedom and power as the dogmatic basis for reforming the church.

Costly, Progressive discipleship of the reforming African–American church in the world come of age challenged the European–American church's cheap grace, both Fundamentalist and Liberal, with an indestructible faith worth imitating. Through this church, God taught faith as a victory overcoming the world. Jesus' words in John 16.33 are also in 1 John 5.3–5. "For God's love consists in keeping God's orders, which are not burdensome, for whatever God gives birth to conquers the cosmos and our faith is the victory that overcomes the cosmos. Who is the one who overcomes the cosmos but the one who believes Jesus is God's Son?" (My translation.) This church was an act of faith bringing people into empowering contact with God in Christ, the source of all power (*Against,* 273, 275 and *Palestine,* 145). He transcended the interpretation Wilmore wrote about, challenging people greater progress under God's Gospel than unjust, abusive owners and after Emancipation, oppressors; but not just them, but Fundamentalist, Liberal, emotivist, rationalist, immoral and indifferent Africans, too (beyond *Black Witness,* 12). While Wilmore found that, in the main, most African churches either called parishioners to costly discipleship or protested abuses and injustices, Powell did both. His twist of Pascal's wager bet his life that God existed and that Jesus His Son came to save him through His life and death (*Palestine,* 131). The faith that overcomes the cosmos was Progressive and revolutionary, transcending all definitions and limitations.

The sermon Powell preached most often is "The Model Church," the first congregation, in Jerusalem, aware of sins, repenting in and through faith (129, 131f), acting and committing, not to a belief or intellectual agreement (Ibid). Shannon said practice without praise is humanism; praise without practice was theosophy. Theology was action before abstract reflection, (*Black Witness,* 7 and *The Old Testament Experience of Faith,* 15f). Powell asserted that the ideal church gave five gifts to Africans. Organizational techniques, space for the grace of an equal social plane, community leadership, experience rehearsing the meekness of Jesus and an emotional outlet were the gifts the Church bestowed on African people (*Upon This Rock,* 107, 109, 111–113, *Against,* 276). The recognition of people as social beings, made by God for society, was his ideal church's mandate (Welty, 73).

The concept of equality through interpreting egalitarian Biblical texts, practicing Spiritual Biblical interpretation, is the meat of chapter two. Emotionalization of the ideal of Christ–like universal love as a key hermeneutical principle is the stuff of chapter three. The principle of the universal, equalizing love and meekness of Jesus, the centerpiece of his work and life is chapter four's reason for being. Kidd's exaltation of emotionalization of the ideal of Christ–like love, egalitarian goal and key role for women is chapter three.

In New Haven, before Kidd's World War One epiphany, Powell began reforming the church. He realized how liberating and empowering a well–organized church was and how important women were, equal in all respects to men. Robert Austin Warner recalled some of his reforms in Immanuel Church, New Haven. He paid off the debt, installed a costly pipe organ, and attracted many new members by the year 1900. At that time the church had more than 200 members, $18,000 (1900 valuation), clear of debt and European–American financial control (Warner, *New Haven Negroes, a Social History,* 170f, taken from Powell's *Souvenir*, 11f). Warner said Immanuel Church became New Haven's richest and biggest African church because of Powell (171), while Powell said his ministry there was a learning experience. He learned a well–organized church needed not the fund–raising presence of the preacher every week. Absent from Immanuel as long as six weeks, he noted no difference to speak of in collections (*Against*, 136, Welty, 24f). The reform of the church involved key lay leaders. The ministry centered on Jesus Christ and not on Powell. He emphasized the stewardship of the people's gifts and not making people totally dependent on the preacher's gifts. When he took the call to Abyssinian, he set four objectives. As at Immanuel, to create a model church, meaning the Jerusalem church of the Book of the Acts of the Apostles, to teach punctuality, to establish better race relations and to establish the kingdom of social justice on earth (*Rock,* 51f) Jesus had only one church in the United States free enough to follow Him. Rich men or large political machines or businesses dominated European–American churches' preaching and policies. Jesus got a hearing and a following from a humble, unshackled, unbossed African–American church (*Palestine*, 107). Cheap grace was the European–American churches' major problem (Op cit, 52f), creating a tangled web of apostasy in American Christianity ("The Negro's Enrichment," 74). A lack of discipleship and the accommodating of the church to the hypocrisy, racism and greed of European–American society were outcomes of cheap grace. Like Douglass, he opposed machine ecclesiastics in favor of the Book of Acts' ideal church ("Douglass," 339). The ideal Church lived in a world come of age, ecumenical and united (*Palestine,* 31). The world come of age no longer appreciated the creeds and confessions of the church but actions (*Against*, 63). Most people cared not for church doctrines but looked for practical translation of Jesus' Spirit in members' daily lives (Op cit, 64). Every Christian had the keys to open and close the gates of heaven; he and Douglass believed

("Douglass," 340). The virtues costly discipleship inculcated in the church included love, veracity, long–suffering, patience and meekness, drilling them into people in Sunday School and homes ("Enrichment," 73f). The question of the world come of age the church had to answer was what can we do make the world happy? What can we contribute to the uplift of the masses of humanity? (*Palestine,*187.) What did this mean to Bonhoeffer? Geffrey Kelly and Burton Nelson, Editors, found important traces of his answer in their work: *A Testament to Freedom: The Essential Writings of Dietrich Bonhoeffer,* 98, 184, 322ff, 325ff, 532, 535 and 568. Powell's emotionalization of the ideal program worked.

Powell distinguished between Capitalism and democracy. Even Capitalism must bow before God's wrath, the "democratic cyclone" that was the cutting edge of true Progress in the world (*Riots,* 100). The Baptist church best exemplified democracy, with local autonomy and only survived in democracy, he felt. Equalizing democracy correlated the point of contact between the costly grace of Jesus and the world come of age because Jesus came back from the future to transform the world in every present moment now. His goal in changing from Pacifism during the First World War to support the United Nations in the Second was to free Africans in the U. S. and make a world in which weak people fulfill the task Paul gives the church in Philippians 2.12: "My beloved people, just as you always have obeyed me, therefore, not only in my presence, but even more in my absence, work out your own salvation with fear and trembling" (My translation), in his "Tolerance in Race and Religion," (*Riots,* 114). Persecuting Jews means Hitler opposed God (*Riots,* 100). Hitler's dastardly, cowardly treatment of defenseless Jews made him a despicable skunk and cur, permanently weakening Germany because they supported the cheapest ever Biblical interpretation, the holocaust (98), a colossal blunder against unarmed, unorganized people, so God wrote Ichabod over Berlin skies (99, interpreting 1 Samuel 2.32, 3.11fff, 4.19ff), Ichabod meant *no glory* (Pauline Viviano in David N. Freeman, Editor, *The Anchor Bible Dictionary*, Volume 3, 356). One focal point of his ministry opposed persecutions of the weak. He had four struggles in his career that he felt somewhat victorious about; political, social, moral and feeding the hungry (*Against,* 220). Failure to win the struggle against apathy plagued him to the end (*Palestine,* 74f).

In a famous sermon delivered at an NAACP convention in New York, "Dry Bones," Powell wove Ezekiel 34 with texts from the gospels according to John and Matthew 25. He preached that the lack of dis–cipleship, worship services, prayer, reading the Bible, Christian work and feeding on the means of grace, Baptism and the Lord's Supper did not bode well for solving and overcoming poverty, immorality, social injustice and similar issues (117). Jesus, life's fountainhead, yielded a church that is a reservoir of life. In harmony with the reforms Douglass, Harris, Kidd, Papini and Durant advocated, power flowed from Jesus through the Spirit to disciples. They took the fellowship and service of Christ to others, including them in fellowship and service (109).

Powell was a merciful interpreter of the Bible without partiality or hypocrisy. Binding up the fallen, visiting and helping the afflicted, empowering the powerless, he was a spiritual, Progressive interpreter. An open–minded, ecumenical interpreter, socially and emotionally ethical if not always, in his self–confessed immoral methods, he was a loving interpreter. Concern about the conditions of the poor and oppressed drove him to work hard, often to the detriment of his health.

Going beyond Christendom itself to another level of Progressive reformation, Powell interpreted the revelation of God through some of the challenges Durant spelled out in a synoptic, heavily biased *Story of Philosophy* (Durant, *Story of Philosophy,* 484ff). He imagined himself as an enthusiastic amateur who loved life and wanted to practice human teaching, pouring warmth and blood into the fruits of scholarship (xv). His treatments of philosophers were harsh on rationalists and favorable toward intuitionists. Regards were for his mentor, Bertrand Russell (484ff). Raymond Frey noted that Russell was the only exception to stagnant philosophers for Durant, who debated Russell in 1927. He wrote that Russell put forth ideas boldly; risking imprisonment for his Pacifist, Socialist views (Frey, 62). Russell was jailed for Pacifist demonstrations against Britain's entry into World War One (113). Like Russell, Durant advocated a less narrow, broader, open–ended education system based on the principle of continual growth like John Dewey, of Columbia University, Durant's alma mater, believed and taught. Dewey served on the NAACP Board and worked with Powell in the extension campus at Abyssinian. Powell kept growing and learning until his death (noted Rudwick, "The Niagara Movement," in *The Making of Black America,* on Dewey's influence, see *Adam,* 25, 37, his father's continual growth and changing, 11). So did Durant, rebel against structural social Darwinism in 1914 (*Philosophy and the Social Problem,* 1917, 270). His passion for stimulating ordinary people intellectually moved him to envision a church reformation to organize the intelligence of the masses as to their moral obligation, especially through democracy's hope to alleviate human misery (270f). He asks five rhetorical questions of clergy. He challenges clergy to focus their work on organizing human intelligence under the direction of a Philosophical Society, a concept reflecting the subsuming of religious and theological studies under the department of Philosophy in U.S. colleges and universities. They would study the books and gain the knowledge that equipped them for membership in the Society of the Intelligent, to stir up the seeker spirit in everyone who comes to church, incite them to read the Society's reports religiously and spread abroad the material they learn from the Society. He wants their work, minds, commitment, facilities, money, all to support the universal friendship Jesus passionately preached. Understanding each other is a fine way to teach people how to love one another (271). He blissfully replaced Tradition in his native Catholic Church with the Society, unaware of the radical authority of the Bible and Spirit of God over Protestants. He seemed unaware that his model for the Philosophical faculty giving texts to participants replaced the Bishop and his Priests, or the Monastery and their missionary monks. His concepts differed. Evil was inability to see that which is, not overt acts of prejudice and oppression. The cause of charity and social salvation was clarity, while the function of understanding is converting justice into mercy (485f). He waxed on, evangelistically trying to energize clergy and philosophers to become Activists like Russell, who said, "If Europe and America kill themselves off in war it will not necessarily mean the destruction of the human species, nor even an end to civilization." (486.) Russell for Durant, was what Douglass was for Powell, better a Christian than nominal Christians because he was warm, with almost mystic tenderness for people. The two corollaries of growth that produce a new, natural morality were the principle of reverence promoting individuals and communities and the principle of tolerance so the growth of one was not at the expense of others (483f) Powell knew the principles from experience and study before Russell and Durant found them. He gladly wove them into the fabric of his homiletics. For him, reverence = Piety, which put humble doers of righteousness in touch with the source of universal power. He knew worship empowered people. Costen knew a church received strength from God's saving power, the resurrection being its epitome. Thereby the community faced perils, endured struggles. God's protective power made it all possible (Costen, 118). She knew what Powell also knew, that through God in worship, people solved problems and overcame giant struggles (*Palestine*, 142). The meek method of overcoming evil powers, he believed, came from Jesus was not just Christian. No Fundamentalist said what he said about Gandhi as the greatest incarnation of moral power in the universe (442). Gandhi was in a favorite sermon interpreting the four times in the book of Joshua that God said, "Be strong and of good courage and none shall be able to stand before you." (189, Joshua 1.6f , 9 and 18.) Reverence powered people to achieve a vital tolerance, sensitive to the needs of others. Durant pleaded with a European–American audience for something Powell's flock also needed, tolerance. He struggled for more than tolerance, however: To change perceptions of his people from messengers from Satan to God's image in ebony ("Douglass," 342). That change led to new peace and happiness for all sides. He reformed the church to expand services of prayer, preaching and person–to–person evangelism, Christian education and international mission (*Against,* 169). The first church in Jerusalem according to Acts carried the church to people, so he reckoned every church member must do the same (*Palestine,* 135).

Joseph Johnson gave the same mandate in the 1970s. The very center of the Christian faith was evangelism, since every Christian exists for others. The mission of every member was bringing others into the fellowship by sharing what each one finds in Jesus with others (*Proclamation,* 154). European–American theologians concerned the secular city with God's message and action, while African neighbors directed God's message and action to overcome the realities of stubborn slum captivity and all the dimensions and facets of victimization by racism and outright oppression. They also addressed the financially secure, few Africans in their seduction by economic and educational success to believe they escaped racist subtleties and distance themselves from the masses who struggled just to live (155, addressing Harvey Cox, who wrote *The Secular City* in 1965). Progress and evangelism were the same element for Powell, whose sermon, "Progress–The Law of Life," asserted God's woe to those at ease in church (Zion), quoting what God says to Joshua about urging people to go forward. The church as a place of constant activity stemmed from the principle that inaction means death, action means life. Going backward, trying to stay the same, or recreate the past, was death (Amos 6.1 and Exodus 14.15 in *Against,* 167f). Prayer and Bible study comprised the energy core of the church (*Riots,* 93). Prayer as the greatest freedom in the world, and every act of his ministry, stemmed from his unshakable belief that God heard and answered prayer (*Against,* 165, 285). Praying in the Bible turned the Spirit of the Biblical text into spiritual food (*Palestine,* 95). Prayer kept hope's fire burning today no less than in slaves' souls for centuries (*Riots,* 93).

The kind of prayerful hermeneutics Powell described were set out in organized pattern by Bishop Johnson's father, also a Christian Methodist

Episcopal preacher. He lacked the theological education his son possessed. Johnson called his father's prayerful interpretation method, "wrestling with the Scriptures." His father advocated Spiritual susceptibilities like those of Harris: Devotion and prayer. Reading through the entire book of the Bible in which the text is found came next and paying attention to the material leading up to and following after the text followed. Exploring the problems and situation of the people in the story came before oral reading of the text, which allowed the preacher to hear the text and allow it to address her or him personally. Discover both the divine and the human elements in the situation and text. The exegete must experience and feel what the writer and participants experienced and felt, and use his or her imagination to put one's self in the text's situation, assuming the roles of the story's characters, acting as though one is present among the first audience to hear the story (why not among those who lived it?). Ask the text what the Lord's message of healing and renewal is for the people who will participate in the sermon. Wait for God to communicate. The preacher then begins slow, rises high, strikes fire and sits down (46f). Costen took the matter from the Spiritual hermeneutics of the Puritans and African culture, stating that people who pray (Pray–ers > Prayers, Costen, 106) were empty cisterns open to sacred power enabling them to enter the sacred altar and say what needs saying.

The approach is not limited to romantic Puritans and African–Americans. Justo and Catherine Gonzalez use a similar approach (*Liberation Preaching*, 69–93). After World War I, K. Barth's energies move toward looking into and beyond the historical situation into the spirit of the Scriptures, the Holy Spirit and into an uninterrupted conversation between yesterday's and tomorrow's wisdom (*The Epistle to the Romans*, 1). Their appeal for progress in sanctifying power over and against the racism of European–American and the demons in Europe that immediately started working until Third Reich and the Second World War manifested the loss of moral character Powell thought inevitable when prayer and a personal God were abandoned (*Riots*, 95). Personality and character resulted from prayer, Douglass was a prime example. He prayed for many years for God to free him from slavery, finding God's answer when he engaged his legs in the enacted prayer of taking the Underground Railway out of Baltimore ("Douglass," 341 and *Against,* 165). Faith wove prayer, moral fiber with social progress and fed on preached words of God and sacrament.

Another witness to the scarcity of Powell's sort of reformer was

August Meier, a product of professional higher education (*Negro Thought in America, 1880–1915: Radical Ideologies in the Age of Booker T. Washington,* 221). Powell worshiped education, not slavishly; he reformed education, too. Harris was academic. Kidd, Papini and Durant were outside academe. They shared features, including an appreciation for the power of emotion's place in ethics, following the likes of David Hume. Only a handful of African–American clergy had this kind of awareness and hermeneutics, Meier opined.

On emotions and ethics, Sidney Cornelia Callahan feels emotions energize and adapt, increase effective communication, social bonding and problem–solving, the emotions of love and sympathy create the bonds and contexts that make, care for, educate and socialize new and different sorts of people. Such emotionalized social ethics ensure social groups' very being (*In Good Conscience: Reason and Emotion in Moral Decision Making,* 101). She followed, one way or another, in his steps. In prayer, he spoke to God in the language of Matthew 7.7, "Ask and you will receive, seek and you will find." God decided, in history, that the destinies of European and African people wove together in the United States ("Douglass," 342 and *Palestine,* 173f and 179). From interpreting, feeling and praying through the Scriptures came the struggle for the equality of women with men in his ministry and mission ("Social," 15). Also, supplying social and spiritual needs was important (*Against,* 221). The first preachers Jesus called were so imbued with the Spiritual message, prayer and feeling of supplying the masses' real needs that they organized and shared what they had with the poor (*Palestine,* 115, based on The Acts of the Apostles). Callahan believed one continuous history from Hebrew prophets to civil rights and struggles for liberation exists as moral indignation and anger sparking new horizons of freedom. Empathy for excluded groups, including slaves, women, abused children, laborers, physically challenged, institutionalized patients initiates moral revolutions. The fine, careful perception that opposes stereotypes, mechanical dismissals, and habitual, inert, careless argumentation comes from love motives (Callahan, 132, also Justin Oakley, *Morality and the Emotions,* 189f). Social developments, cultural progress, all derive from emotionalizing the ideal of love, a religious virtue, empathizing across lines of exclusion.

Ernst Kaesemann addressed the European churches' need for another reformation, asking the question of spiritual and ethical integrity in reforming the church from his standpoint as a New Testament scholar. What happens to a church whose devout members stop being liberal and whose liberals stop being devout? (Kaesemann, *Jesus Means Freedom,*

20.) Powell did not tolerate Spiritual schizophrenia, in whose reformation divine condemnation was avoidable and everlasting life attainable, not in some distant future heaven but in every present moment in which we believe and do the proclaimed Word of the Lord (*Palestine*, 167). His spirituality simply consisted in believing, telling and living the truth. Highbrow intellectualizing was spiritually inane as lowbrow emotivism for him ("Old Time Religion," 19).

Renita Weems wrote of her Spiritual hermeneutical motive that Biblical scholars work as much from faith as from feats of learning. She stubbornly had faith that small, persistent, subordinate actions eventually topple the powers of oppression, her reformation of church, not at all unlike Powell's ("Womanist Reflections on Biblical Hermeneutics," in *Documentary History, Volume 2*, 222).

A warning to European and European-American Churches that a further, more radical reformation must occur came from Franz Overbeck (1837-1905), the reformation Powell, Callahan and Weems, among others, work to achieve. He believed all Christians since Eusebius the Arian historian, subsumed faith under the authority of the states and cultures of Western Civilization, denied its eschatological essence, making it Satanic and unchristian (cited by K. Barth, *Romans*, note 2, 3). Powell reformed the church in accord with God's eschatological demands as present discipleship, pushed the traditional beyond the boundaries of cheap grace parochialism and provincialism. He went beyond the boundaries Overbeck and Barth noted in league with Kaesemann, who lamented the cultural captivity of the German church, the limitation of preserving, strengthening and increasing internal order under the control of traditional social and political forms which made all revolution anti-Christian (Kaesemann, 12). Post-World War II Germany and European-America shared a common problem. The holocaust and the War happen when we imagine Jesus in our own image, misinterpreting in the most mawkish fashion his relationship with sinners and glossing over his terrifying, stern judgment as a consuming fire and sword, hiding his freedom and possibly, his rebellion (29). The Viet Nam War razed the image of a so-called free world for him. The Ku Klux Klan in the United States and Nazis in the holocaust were aspects of the Western captivity of the Church for which we were responsible (34f). When Powell stated that the African-American Church consistently opposed lynching, he included the European churches as well as U. S. churches among those who did not. His reformation hoped the Holy Spirit created and recreated the Church (*Palestine*, 142, 144). The freedom of God's children came from the Holy Spirit, the mysterious power that heralded and accomplished it (15).

God owns people because God makes them through race birth and grace birth (113f). God waits to give the Spirit to empty–hearted, asking people, his exegesis of Matthew 5.3, "Blessed are the poor in spirit, the kingdom of heaven is theirs" (my translation) (*Against,* 271). The Spirit brings about meekness and non–resistance, Matthew 5.9f, 21–26 and 43–48 (Op cit, 114). For him, God's words are spirit and life, John 1.3f ("Rocking," 12). Feeling the Holy Spirit is the greatest experience on earth, John 1.12f, 33 (Op cit, 113). The Holy Spirit keys emotional and intellectual progress. The church draws complete, total healing from the Holy Spirit. Costen agrees, as God's story features the defeat of evil powers of suffering and oppression and healing and wholeness for people lead lives full of Spiritual meaning. These facts are celebrations that meet psychological needs and empower constructive, liberating social and cultural action. Her people cope because of what Powell called the Spiritual resurrection from sin to new life in grace birth (Costen, 123 and "Rocking," 124). Because of the Spirit, people laugh, cry, testify, pray, work, walk, run, shout, leap like the man in Acts 3 who waits at Beautiful Gate for someone to put him in the pool; all along, he just needs the power of the Spirit. Reformation of the church to make social, multicultural progress rested on a prophetic–Spiritual interpretation of the Bible, open to new revelations from God in experience. Sometimes new revelations came from God through critics of the church. Powell did not welcome all reforms; he excluded Fundamentalism, unbridled emotivism, intellectualism and Liberalism. Abstract reasoning in the pulpit and jazzed–up Spirituals were unwelcome. Kaesemann noted that the intellectual argument the Reformation spawned is dull as a household routine and hermeneutical inconstancy one of the Reformed Church's constants (Kaesemann, 35), not liberating, empowering action.

The Spirituals took the place for Powell of dogmatic theology in the Reformed tradition and the Lutheran, and that John Wesley's sermons play among Methodists and the Articles of Religion among Anglicans. He resisted changing this sacred music, his hermeneutic norm– the Spiritual. Costen and Cone thought the human spirit found freedom for God's Spirit to penetrate and intensify God's powerful presence through singing. Music as the Spirit, free to move, unordered, created a mood of freedom, openness to the quickening awareness of God, hearing and receiving grace (Costen, 45, Cone, *Speaking the Truth,* 25).

Human progress hinged in part on reforming the church along Pro–gressive lines. Powell turned to various authors, academic and non–academic, churchly and non–churchly. Their visions of progress all arrived at the eschatological principle of equalizing democracy through deepening the emotions of sympathy and love. Spirituality commits to harmony in African studies (Asante, 172f, 179ff). Harmony does not exist without equality, unless harmony is, explicitly or inherently, a form of inequality. Hiring Virginia Wood as Abyssinian's first female Youth Director was his career's crowning achievement (*Against*, 268ff).

For Powell, harmony was the goal replacing the hell of inequality in us with heavenly equanimity in the present. The progressive church enabled us to live, not only for the sake of future egalitarian harmony, says he, but in the present. A few examples: power entrusted to lay leaders, bestowing credit for excellence on Assistant Ministers, appreciation of Burroughs's work and the crowning achievement of 1936, his last year as Pastor of Abyssinian Church, appointing a woman to direct his youth ministry. He worked for practical equality in the present because of Biblical promises he interpreted spiritually. Not many African–American preachers in his day were Progressive prophets. Lawrence Maningo and C. Eric Lincoln found only a few preachers taking stands to meet the needs of poor people in the 1920s. Powell opened one of the first Soup Kitchens in the roaring twenties in the community where the church built a new facility. His social outreach was the exception, not the rule (C. Eric Lincoln and Lawrence H. Maningo, *The Black Church in the African–American Experience,* 121),

Welty recognized Powell's belief that the church in a world come of age had a moral duty to act meaningfully in everyday life in his early, vigorous fulfillment of the Social Gospel (Welty, 24). His Social Gospel owed more to Harris, however, than to Rauschenbusch, rooted in Douglass's description of the true church of the faith of Jesus caring for sick, wounded, distressed and poor people, going into the gutters and streets to find them every day (25, 1906, "The Significance of the Hour"). His church was no socially and politically silent Fundamentalist or Liberal one in 1906, the year Bonhoeffer was born. Since Welty, Clark, Kinney and Hamilton did not write about his pragmatic advocacy of the liberation of women in concert with Burroughs, my effort at least corrects their omission. His horizon of Progress rose higher than most and exceeded the freedom horizon of newcomers Barth and Bonhoeffer.

Chapter Six

Powell's Hermeneutics and Beyond

The foregoing study of Powell's hermeneutics in the intellectual context he chooses shows similarities and dissimilarities between him and his sources. I confront the racist stereotyping of European and European–American academe that caricatures Powell as an emotivistic, Fundamentalist, revival preacher and cordons off the emotionalization of the ideal of the universal love of Jesus from any intellectual content in his work or in the experience of his hospitality by Bonhoeffer. My theory is that Bonhoeffer does not analyze his Abyssinian experience as he analyzes European–American churches because he internalizes Powell's theology. His future as an interpreter of African–American theology does not remain unfulfilled. Throughout his work, especially *The Cost of Discipleship*, he is the best German interpreter of African–American theology. When K. Barth inserts *Nachfolge* into *Church Dogmatics*, African–American theology enters into post–modern Western Christendom and the hermeneutic circle is broken open from within. Not as free as he or Barth could be, but six months is not enough time to experience the full force of Powell's completely liberating theology, especially by one whose freedom transcends African Patriarchal culture as well as Fundamentalist exclusivity. He shares a common tradition with Douglass's and Harris's hermeneutics. Bercovitch observes that the evolution of Puritan hermeneutics from the Colonial era onward hinges on symbolic logic, which allows new and different kinds of interpreters and contexts through interaction between the interpreters and the facts, providing the interpreter identifies oneself as spiritually born–again. Since that claim can be an act of imagination and will, new interpreters are free to claim that their interpretations incarnate the true and only America (Bercovitch, 185). The subjective basis for participation in the

American conversation means, in reality, that any interpretation that enables a given person or group to live deserves tolerance. From that standpoint, in the context of transplantation and oppression, Powell's interpretation of Scripture stands or falls according to the criterion of pragmatic harmonization. Are people free and powerful to equalize their place in the United States through deepening the emotions of sympathy and love in their oppressors or not? Not only does this issue rise from his first article, "Douglass," but from his autobiography, *Against*. Does he open the hermeneutic circle he shares with Douglass and Harris? The question's answer lies in experience and reality, not in books.

The chapters before show that Powell distances his work, as does Harris and Papini, from rationalism, emotivism, Fundamentalism, Liberalism and other alternatives that do not affect egalitarian, universal love. Sometimes I wish emotional worship alone draws Bonhoeffer to Abyssinian, as Zerner, Young and Wind guess, but Young comes closest, regretting to me that he does not have my research at his disposal when he writes his book. He tells me, "No Harlem, no Bonhoeffer." He is right, but the real subject is not only Harlem, but Powell. Harris advocates his own brand of New England hermeneutics, probably the last of an old breed. He opens the hermeneutical circle for African–American hermeneutics and establishes a distinctive conception of the place of intuition and emotion in hermeneutics. The African Spiritual tradition in the Spirituals breaks the hermeneutic circle open for one who differs in many ways to create a circle of influence all his own.

The African religion, culture and society are his standpoint, not Harris's. The Spirituals comprise his theological dogmatics. An empty heart and mind as a precondition for authentic Biblical interpretation, deriving from the first Beatitude in Matthew 5, poor in spirit. Practical reconciliation, empowering and liberating of all people starting with Africans is his immediate goal. A radical concept of miracles in history meeting and changing whatever scientists claim is determined by history and an overwhelming drive toward universal harmony through the emotionalization of the ideal of Jesus Christ's universal love. He set out to create an ideal, model church, the most valuable gift of Christianity to Africans. He assaults every cheap grace form of the faith of Jesus and calls on a jaded, indifferent world come of age to fulfill a moral duty to uplift the masses of the people starting with the poor and oppressed and focusing on the liberating of women. A recent partner in this kind of hermeneutics is Itumeleg Mosala (in his *Biblical Hermeneutics and Black Theology in South Africa*, 1989, 173–193) and many Womanist theologians including Grant, Weems and Delores Williams.

Most African–American preachers in his day are Fundamentalists and emotivists. Some are rationalist and a few are Liberal. Progressive means his theology and hermeneutics are polyphonic and rare. He works on several goals simultaneously, and while this creates burn–out problems for him, it demonstrates his high sense of moral duty. One goal is real human moral progress, contingent on changing European–American perceptions of African people as messengers from the devil into messengers from God in shades of black. The closed circle is open by means of a progressive morality that is older than the Gospel of Wealth and more Christian, Timothy Smith thinks (he and Richard Lambert edit, *Religion in American Society–American Academy of Political and Social Sciences,* November, 1960, 15). Powell realizes that whether African churches are Fundamentalist, Liberal, charismatic or intellectual, they oppose Capital punishment and promote interracial unity more persistently than those of Europe or New England. They are still the only churches capable of hearing Jesus in any authentic fashion, as long as they are free from European, Capitalist or phony African–American middle class control. As Juan Luis Segundo maintains, the closed hermeneutical circle is an inevitable product of Greco–Roman philosophies and can be broken into through fidelity to what he and other Catholics call Tradition, but which Powell and Scheler assert is the free and freeing voice of God speaking through the Bible (Segundo in William Ferm, Editor, *Third World Theologies: A Reader,* 88). He is not as optimistic about biological/evolutionary progress as Harris, much less so the ultra–rational Bascom. If he lives long enough, will Harris change, like Kidd or Papini? With them, Powell's eschatology is more radically futurist and transforming of the present than Harris's. He does not subscribe to the old pie–in–the–sky religion, no matter what Hamilton thinks (Hamilton, 80, 85, where he uses the very words, and he is supposed to be a historian). On the contrary, his interpretation of the eschatology of Jesus aims to displace hell with heaven in people and society in this and every present moment now until God calls him home. The present moment is the future of reconciliation, freedom and power and the state of the historic struggle for freedom, power and equality for all. The most remarkable difference between them is his different content for the category of spiritual susceptibility. Papini reads the Gospel many times, but with a hostile spirit until the terrors of the First World War transform him, liberating him through Tolstoy and Dostoyevsky, the Russian novelists, and the Sermon on the Mount to hear and proclaim the Gospels, but limits the universal love of Jesus under Tuscan cultural and social denigrations of women and Jews. Ultimately, he falls prey to

Fascism. When Powell discovers the conservative wing controls the Republican Party of Theodore Roosevelt to which he belongs and which elects him the first African member of the Electoral College, he freely changes Party membership, criticizing Roosevelt's cousin, Franklin, as he endeavors to actualize his older cousin's political vision.

Bercovitch finds that the interpreter must be regenerate; not so for Powell. Regeneration comes before, after and only through the event of the Spirit transforming the Bible reader through the Bible. After all, his conversion involves the sound of silence. Whose spiritual susceptibility determines entry into the hermeneutical circle?

African–American Psychologist Roderick Pugh notes how his classmates in his African Methodist Episcopal Sunday School blush when their teacher reads The Song of Solomon 1.5–6: "I am black and beautiful, O daughters of Jerusalem, like the tents of Kedar, like the curtains of Solomon. Do not stare at me because I am dark, because the sun has gazed on me." They are victims of the Simon Lagree system, internalizing their history's irrelevance to the dominant culture's general hermeneutic circle and hate their skin color (Pugh, *Psychology and the Black Experience,* 1972, 18).

Finally, Powell rejects Harris's notion of miracles as harmonious extensions of the natural and determined. That is too evolutionary (slow) a social hermeneutics of conversion and change. He changes from hoodlum to Christian, after all. The miraculous will of God meets and transforms the natural, biological hermeneutical circle that denies even the existence of him and his people. Segundo thinks we may expect completion and correction of the road toward liberation from Biblical passages in the future, but adapts that future struggle to Darwinian categories like Chardin and almost like Bascom (*Third World,* 88), not very different from Bultmann who subsumes interpretation under Heidegger's Parmenides program. Bultmann breaks with the Third Reich only when they arrest his brother. The debates between Gutierrez and Segundo mirror the debate between Cone, who is more with Powell, Barth and Gutierrez than Johnson, like Bultmann, Segundo and Chardin.

Spiritual interpretation as a philosophical, intellectual category that subsumes scientific, form–critical study in open–hearted Bible reading facilitates part of Powell's growing, changing career. What Kidd sees as the next stage in the social evolution of Anglo–Saxons, educating poor working class people benefits Powell, who takes over the mission and advocates a step further up the road to moral progress. He does not allow formal learning to interfere with education any more than he allows Fundamentalism, conservatism, Liberalism or racism to interfere with his continuing formal education and rigorous reading and study. Evolutionary change as the early Kidd posits rationalizes Anglo–Saxon superiority; what else can alter monolithic power except a miracle? Racism is official American academic and national policy. When Powell asks the biological sociologists to wait before passing final judgment on Africans, he is not accepting racism, but challenges racism by advocating a special, powerful mission African people uniquely carry out. He struggles against monism for pluralism; only a miracle can change the situation. The wholism of Chardin seems wonderful until the snail–slow pace of Darwinian social change rears its ugly head.

The problems of individualism and violent disposition that destroy Anglo–Saxons and Germans require a miracle, according to Kidd, to affect change. Powell advocates the miraculous solution. He agrees with Kidd that information emotionalizing people under the ideal of universal sympathy and love is a hermeneutical criterion with mental organization being a power serving the common good. His reading of William James, Durant, Harris, Kidd, Freud and others inform his awareness of the relation between emotion and ethics, social and personal. He resonates with Kidd's egalitarian, anti–monopolist, altruist emotion and religion. The collectivist values Kidd propounds accord well with those of American progressives. He foreshadows such later positivists of emotion and intuition as Henri Bergson, Carl Jung and Chardin (Crook, 2). Does this mean Bergson has to renounce his Judaism and that Jung has to favor Nazism and that Chardin has to bow theology's head to Darwin? African–Americans rebel against those who insist on taking everything away from them. Powell experiences Anglo–Saxons who expect to steal more while giving nothing. He is aware of Anglo–American scholars saying Egyptians are white–skinned; travel in Egypt showing him the truth about the Nubian Egyptians (*Against*, 133).

How can an African–American criticize problems within European–American culture with integrity? As a messenger of meekness, an emotionalizing angel God sends who can demonstrate, boycott, march and agitate for progressive changes. Less optimistic about scientific hermeneutics from Strauss to Renan than Kidd, he is more like Papini, but, with Kidd, unapologetic about African emotionality. From expecting social change to occur without upsetting the British apple cart, Kidd realizes that without a miracle, conflict is inevitable. While Powell works hard to achieve peaceful, harmonic social change, he unhesitatingly pens an apology for disenchanted, rioting African–Americans (*Riots,* and Capeci, *The Harlem Riot of 1943*, 18f and 66).

Professor emeritus Rubem Alves moves from Fundamentalism

through dialectical Neo–orthodoxy to disenchantment with what the U.S. does to overthrow Salvador Allende in Chile. Now he expounds on Scheler and Nietzsche again. He struggles with humans humanizing nature, impregnating nature with the future, transforming the physical universe into a downward turn of love, the *ordo amoris* of Scheler ("From Paradise to Desert," in *Third World,* 107). How will he resolve the conflict between Nietzsche's rejection of the *ordo amoris* in favor of the will to power and Scheler's phenomenology?

Powell risks rejection and death on all sides as he puts into practice the universal goal of multi–racial, or, as we say, multi–cultural unity. That he takes the heat and achieves results shows that his principles are neither theoretical nor rhetorical. Rather, he is deeply, spiritually committed to the promised harmony of God. With Papini, Powell saves society through the universal application of Jesus' law of love. Scheler's *ordo amoris*, or something more free and joyful than he or Papini think?

Harris and Powell are clergy in non–creedal traditions (Congregational and Baptist). Unlike the Catholic Papini and lapsed Catholic Durant, Harris and he have no official church creeds and dogmas over their religious content. Like Harris and him, Papini experiences his faith journey in social and personal suffering. The question begs answering: Is Papini's relationship to Catholic dogmatics all that conforming?

Can suffering ever comfortably be shut out of a hermeneutic circle unless built on some kind of cruelty–whether of an old Thomism that castrates a secretly married Peter Abelard or an old Calvin burning a heretic at the stake or Puritans burning witches and destroying defenseless Native–, African–, Hispanic– and Asian–Americans, or a Teutonic existentialist nihilism burning and shooting millions of Jews, Communists, Labor leaders, physically and mentally challenged people (the first to go), Gypsies, Tinkers, Africans and Christians? How sad, fear–provoking and anger–producing a result of apathy are they?

Harris, Kidd, Papini, Durant and Powell want to change all social institutions according to the principle of universal love. Brotherizing is a better solution to conflict than war, prison or brutality (*Riots,* 112fff, 171), a fine exegesis of the trajectory of relationship–building in Philemon 15f. When youth gangs organize in Harlem, Powell reaches out to charge them with running the gymnasium according to the rules. His son evangelizes the entire leadership of the Black Panther Party into Abyssinian Church in the 1970s. They are experts at making brothers and sisters of rebellious sinners.

The choice facing Kidd, Papini, Durant and Powell in the wake of the First World War is between a divine miracle and nothingness. Is that any different today? Social transformation stops, for Papini, at real equality. The rigid class structure of Italian society stymies upward mob‒bility, a factor in his interpretation of Fascism. Powell favors upward social mobility moderating at equality as practical outcome of social change by the miracle of divine love. The taint of racism Bacon notes in Papini is lacking in Powell. Nonetheless, Powell shares his belief in Jesus elevating people by going among them, affecting a social revolution by changing emotion, reason, intent and action. He affirms, with Papini, the role of Jesus as a practicing over‒turner or reverser of natural expectations. Love of enemies is the *sine qua non* for Papini and Powell, as for Harris. Evidently the phenomenon of everyone going to War is enough justification for Scheler (*The Genius of War and the German War*, 1915 in Victor Farias, *Heidegger and Nazism*, 1989), but not for K. Barth (*Romans*). The First War destroys the realized eschatology claims of Kaiser Wilhelm's Teutonic philosophical and theological hermeneutics and Kidd's Anglo‒Saxon supremacist hermeneutics of 1894. Many people realize the End has not yet come. The reality of the future of Jesus now, but not yet realized, affirms Papini, Powell practices, risking his life. Alves comments on our situation. Gods, demons and religion are limitations of which we feel shame, so we cloak our values and dreams with scientific shams. Life has no certainties except passion, vision and risk (*Third World*, 107).

Powell is more open, with Harris and Kidd, perceiving this force outside Christendom, citing the Hindu Mahatma, Gandhi, as an example. Papini upsets the Catholic Church by applying the universal law of love to transforming the devil. This point resonates with Powell's altering of Anglo‒American opinions of Africans.

Papini interprets poverty to help the poor as desirable as Ambrose and Augustine. Powell favors such help and organizes the practical help people need. Believing more strongly in equality and the principle of work, he interprets 1 Thessalonians 4.11–12 and 2 Thessalonians 3.10 to preach help, education, work and equality

Since Papini and Powell experience the same Wars on two different shores, their interpretations differ. Papini sees War as an evil that the church supports. Powell sees the First War as wrong and the Second War as a necessary evil that provides opportunity for progressively liberating and empowering Africans (*Palestine*, 69). He echoes sentiments from the editors of *The Age* and *The Crisis* in asking the rhetorical question as to why fight to protect international commerce when Africans experience oppression and suppression of economics in the United States? They assert with one voice that hanging and burning African children and adults without trials in peace is worse than Germans blowing up ships full of molasses and mules (Roi Ottley and William Weatherby, Jr., Editors, *The Negro in New York: An Informed Social History*, 197f).

Papini has a lower view of women that Powell, who is closer to Douglass and the post–War Kidd (*Palestine,* 172f). They commit, however, to justice for the poor and oppressed. He also differs from Papini: He has a greater, more egalitarian regard for Jews. Their grinding poverty in Germany made him realize that Jews are in far worse condition in Europe than Africans in the U. S. of the '20s and '30s. The brothers Bonhoeffer disagree with him (*Against* and Bethge, 110).

Biblical interpretation still wrestles with the same problems as Powell. All attempts to separate the words of God from human words in the Bible are futile. He enjoys and benefits from Biblical interpretation by following energies of texts in relation to adjacent, complementary and contradictory texts and real experiences, especially those texts and experiences that confront and expose shams and lies. Rejecting hermeneutic theories that follow legal (forensic), heroic–romantic, other–worldly, Liberal, Fundamentalist and sentimental programs, he struggles to overcome such mechanical efforts in others and himself through mutually liberating service and enjoyment. He freely responds through Biblical interpretation to a liberating, empowering Lord who enjoys and glorifies people, especially the poor and oppressed. That is why the letterhead of Abyssinian Church proclaims "'The Church of the Masses.'" (*The Negro in New York,* 290.)

Powell never stops reading the Bible. He discovers new truths during his lifetime as surely as new truths appear since 1953. The Bible still reveals. How will Powell write that? Perhaps he will say that the Bible never stops surprising and reading us? That new truths discover us through spirited Bible reading? That the Spirit still discovers new ways to free and empower the children who lie outside the gate, like Segundo and Gutierrez? He knows the practical effects of a Biblical hermeneutics determine appropriateness. Harris, Kidd, Papini and Durant, like him, know all individualistic interpretation is dead in the ash heaps of two World Wars and the Depression. They know, moreover, that all purely rationalist hermeneutical options are as dead as all over–spiritualized and emotive hermeneutics. Vincent Winbush thinks the African–American New Testament interpretation has a sense of the life of the community trying to make encounters with Jesus meaningful, an answer to a form–critic's prayer, providing, in my view, that the philosophy of the form–critic is closer to Scheler, with his *ordo amoris* than to Heidegger's Nihilism (Winbush, "'Rescue the Perishing:' The Importance of Biblical

Scholarship in Black Christianity," in *Documentary History, Vol.2*, 212). Jesus, after all, keeps pushing Powell along a way Kelly Miller describes as the zig–zag path of progress between injustice and justice (Miller, *The Negro in New York*, 291).

Where will hermeneutics go in the future? Sadly, with few exceptions, most European–American and European theologians ignore African– and Latin–American Biblical hermeneutics. Reginald Fuller's "New Testament Theology" cites not one eschatological New Testament hermeneutics except Wolfhart Pannenberg, Juergen Moltmann and Dorothee Soelle, none of them North, Central or South American, Asian, Native– or African–American (Fuller, "New Testament Theology," in Eldon Epp and George MacRae, Editors, *The New Testament and Its Modern Interpreters,* 571). Royce Gruenler takes a neo–Stoic stance, dismisses emotion, or sensation as having a disruptive effect on the rational interpretation of the Bible. He refers to Spiritual regeneration as an act instead of an experience and to the roots of his hermeneutics in Jonathan Edwards without bringing Edwards' criticism of racism and expositions of religious emotions up to date. Why should he deal with the disastrous consequences of European–American hermeneutics in the African– or Native–American holocausts, persecutions of women, Asians, Jews, Germans, Italians, Irish and others? (Gruenler, *Meaning and Understanding: The Philosophical Framework for Biblical Interpretation*, 33ff.) Does a concern for empathy in hermeneutics disappear after Dilthey first imports the science of hermeneutics from theology to develop a sociological hermeneutics, as Antony Flew suggests? (Flew, Editor, "Hermeneutics," *Dictionary of Philosophy.*) Jana Sawicki is on target about de–constructionists, post–structuralists and the race to the next better theory overshadowing and supplanting women, people of color and Third–world authors. Disenchanted European males create post–structural literary theory, which becomes more important than subjugated works of the others about which they write, not surprising her or me (Jana Sawicki, "Foucault and Feminism," in Michael Kelly, Editor, *Critique and Power: Recasting the Foucault/Habermas Debate,* 356f). Even now the ghost of Simon Lagree dictates that only scholars of elite ethnicities write universal stuff.

Patrick Colm Hogan, a disenchanted male, uses Jacques Derrida's hermeneutics to address the cause of his anguish, the U. S. response to the Nicaragua revolution, similar to Alves's and the Chile problem in my earlier segment. Hogan wants an anarchist university in the U. S. (Hogan, *The Politics of Deconstruction: Ideology, Professionalism and the Study of Literature.*) Anarchists deconstruct closed circles of hermeneutics all the time, from early prophets like Amos the Shepherd to Papini, Kropotkin and radicals in Powell's Harlem to Black Panthers in the 1970s (Philip Foner, Editor, *The Black Panthers Speak*). Hogan's and Alves's disenchantment with the closed circle of North American hermeneutics is a broad experience of many. For example, the late David Hirsch puts the problem another way. Fusion of horizons is a code word for hermeneutic circle and results in disembodied, abstract discourses that ignore twentieth–century history and overlook the question of how a post–Auschwitz awareness can fuse horizons with re–presentations of the pre–Auschwitz world that makes future terrors inevitable (Hirsch, *The Deconstruction of Literature*, 218). The multinational corporations of the West ignore international courts and attempts to establish moral principles until after September 11, when they realize their Buccaneer value system allows Terrorists as well as Corporate terrorism and turn to theological ethicists like Bishop Tutu for advice on creating a world of justice and peace governing corporations, too (World Trade Conference, New York, February, 2002).

Bernard Lategan responds to the increasing importance of the pragmatic aspect of Scripture, the result of speech–act, rhetorical–critical, reader studies and contextual theologies (African, Liberation and Feminist), as though Dutch– and English–Africans are not ethnic groups. He thinks Feminist, African and Liberation theologies develop from interest in the persuasive potential of the Bible, as though that potential does not occur in his ethnic group. Any hermeneutical theory, therefore, has a context of reception (Lategan, "Hermeneutics," *The Anchor Bible Dictionary, Vol.3*, 151f). Deconstruction theories of language, holding there is no such thing as communication at all, threatens him and, in fact, all others of his sort who close the circle of meaning by addressing discourse only to a particular audience. This leaves him free to address European–African contexts while avoiding Asian and African contexts. In this scheme the levels of discourse Aristotle arranges according to his hierarchy of beings remains the same and so does every segment of people they categorize.

The impossibility of a mutually liberating, joyful hermeneutics, assumes Karl–Otto Apel. He assails neo–positivism, including New England hermeneutics as Bercovitch parses it as, "a secularized theology of the spirit as derived from Hegel or Schleiermacher," usurping all realms of objectivity. He wants to enable Continental and Anglo–Saxon interpreters to understand one another, which only creates another closed circle of meanings (in Apel, "Perspectives for a General Hermeneutical Theory," in Kurt Mueller–Vollmer, Editor, *The Hermeneutics Reader,*

Texts of the German Tradition from the Enlightenment to the Present, 325). If this is the case, we stand at a much more complex place than Max Weber at the end of the First World War, who stands between the hermeneutics of conviction (religion) and responsibility (political–economic). People expect the political–economic and the religious to change their lives for the better (Ricoeur, *From Text to Action, Essays in Hermeneutics, II,* 336f). The increasing number of people who have nothing to do with any religion at all and who do not vote in elections means that indifference on the one hand and the passivity and complacency of the powers that be on the other hand, conspire to render the causes of groups they disenfranchise impotent and allow Capitalist–ruling belief systems to abuse, categorize, suppress and oppress most people.

Fascist, Marxist and Capitalist options from the arena of secular religion take over for most of the century. Now the hermeneutics of critique (Foucault) expects to change both the arenas of responsibility and conviction, like the Harlem Renaissance critics in Powell's time. At least in the hermeneutics of cynicism the disenchanted think they gain power, whether they do or not. Deconstructionists attack, however, all structures of meaning–nihilism (from Heidegger or Sartre). While this goal draws Asante into cynical hermeneutics, he commits to developing a harmonizing hermeneutics beyond Foucault and neo–naïve Ricoeur (Asante, 179ff).

The debate among philosophers and psychologists of ethics seems to fit within Strawson's categories of resentment and retribution (in Jay Wallace, *Responsibility and the Moral Sentiments,* 10). They argue for rationalism contrary to Watson's interpretation of Strawson's subsuming of religion under political economics, rearranging the deck chairs on the Titanic when what we need is a new ship. If resentment and retribution are all we talk or write about, we still live under the series of deteriorations in communication such limiting options spawn, for example the record of the nihilistic spiral of an Egyptian Pharaoh who does not know or remember Joseph in Exodus 1.8–14, in which his fear of non–being rises to the level of what Heidegger calls an *existentiell* for all beings, entailing the non–being, or demise of Jewish baby boys. Someone asks, in the wake of a war against Terrorism after October 7, 2001, how many people have to die before Americans feel safe?

Someone annihilates six million Jews; someone else bombs innocent Palestinians because religion and economics conspire to allow only the discourses of resentment and retribution. I would rather go with Scheler than with Heidegger–we are essentially social, not loners. Hirsch is onto something when he notes that Martin Buber, building on Jewish foundations and Jacques Maritain (1882–1973), building on an existential Thomism basis see through Heidegger before others, and that Heidegger is a North American problem, especially at Yale, the alma mater of our recent Presidents, one Democrat and the other Republican (Hirsch, 90). Maritain has a religious conversion with a small circle of friends that Leon Bloy (1846–1917) influences and includes artists like Georges Rouault, whose haunting images of Prostitutes and the crucified Jewish (like him) Jesus deeply affect people, all Ernest Hello (1828–1885) fans through Bloy, who oppose racism and anti–Semitism in turn–of–the–century Europe. Maritain's wife, Raissa Oumansoff, a Russian Jewish immigrant, joins her husband's Catholic Church because of Bloy, to deconstruct French Catholic racism and anti–Semitism. Buber sees Heidegger's anti–humanism and despair ultimately subverting personal value. Hirsch thinks Heidegger is the fountain of an "incurable cerebral constipation" (Hirsch, 26 and 266) for philosophers and comparative literary critics in the United States.

I grow up in Oklahoma, where Andrew Jackson sends Native Americans because he is such an Old School Fundamentalist Presbyterian that he believes the world is flat and European–Americans are the only people who get to live on it. European–Americans of Tulsa are so upset over Africans owning oil lands that they steal their properties and burn their neighborhood. I know Nihilism because of Oklahoma. Leonard Jackson knows something about frustration and disenchantment, too, for he knows the hermeneutic circle of phenomenology and existentialism is, "a closed circle of cultural meanings." Meeting an alien culture, unless we find a way to leap intuitively into their circle from some inner experience identifiable by our culture, understanding is impossible. The gulf the circle makes seems breakable only by what Kierkegaard first and L. Jackson now call a, "leap of analytically inexplicable faith." A wedge is driven "between our subjective and objective understandings of the world," which seems "logically impossible to cross at all." (L. Jackson, *The Poverty of Structuralism: Literature and Structuralist Theory*, 258f.) The late James Baldwin says in 1963 that North American popular culture is "based on fantasies created by very ill people ... that have nothing to do with reality." (Baldwin in Rick Simonson and Scott Walker, Editors, *The Graywolf Annual Five: Multi–Cultural Literacy*, 11.) African objective reality is culturally irrelevant, or, as Michele Wallace says invisible. She knows a Cherokee Chief, Wilma Mankiller of Oklahoma. Her struggle with language and representation is invisible to most Oklahomans and

African–Americans like Wallace. She finds the exclusion of Oklahoma from textbooks on American History as fascinating as the nuclear waste dumpsites no one wants to know anything about until September 11, 2001, that is (Wallace, "Invisibility Blues," in *Graywolf*, 171).

If conversation is the only authentic reality for language as structural theorist Hans–Georg Gadamer thinks, does the conclusion necessarily follow that a "fertile fusion of all horizons" is achievable or even desirable? (Gadamer's essay, "Gadamer on Gadamer," in Hugh Silverman, Editor, *Gadamer and Hermeneutics,* 19.) The question remains, can one hand clap?

Ricoeur, still in Heidegger's circle, turns problems into mysteries in so–called fusions that exclude Auschwitz or the North American Red, Black or Yellow holocausts. In spite of being a German Camp during World War Two and introducing K. Barth when The Sorbonne gave a doctorate to him for the quality of his prose after the War. He reminds me of the Bultmann group who say to Barth after the War that they see the Devil in the face of Hitler, to whom he responds that they do not seem to have changed at all. (Hirsch, 217. Also, Jean Amery, *At the Mind's Limits* and Emil Frackenheim, *To Mend the World*).

Keith Oakley revives from Dilthey and Weber the concept of hermeneutics and only sounds like an older Gadamer. Hermeneutics, a fresh import from theology, still insists on achieving empathic, mutual understanding. Factor no party out of the contemporary conversation in our quest for communication. The answer will not come from the state or from religion, in his formulation, although both are factors in the quest for a comprehensive hermeneutics transcending phenomena and measurements, given multiple goals, knowledge limits, ability limits and prior relationships, "to achieve understanding." (Keith Oakley, *Best Laid Schemes: The Psychology of Emotions*, 414f.)

Gary Watson opposes Jay Wallace and Strawson. He cites Gandhi and Martin Luther King, Jr., as rejecting the rhetoric of blame and that of condemnation and still function as moral agents (Watson, "Responsibility and the Limits of Evil, Variations on a Strawsonian Theme," in Ferdinand Schoeman, Editor, *Responsibility, Character and the Emotions, New Essays in Moral Psychology,* 21*).* If holding people responsible entails a moral command and if the attitude shaping the morality derives from retributive feelings which limit good will, then the entire structure of such a system conflicts with the historically powerful emotionalized "ideal of love." Gandhi and King impress Watson as they impress Callahan. They stand up for progress and justice, oppose and confront their oppressors, demand the redress of grievances coming closer than others in similar circumstances to do so without malice or vengeance (Ibid, 537f).

If the late Arthur Cochrane, my theology professor in seminary and Melva Costen, my faculty colleague for eight years teach me correctly, the chief crime for which Christendom must take responsibility is that of driving what Cochrane calls a wedge between the secular and the sacred, the body and the soul, the political and the spiritual, that is foreign to the Bible (Cochrane, *Eating and Drinking with Jesus*, 8). If Biblical hermeneutics is a task in which no one can claim that any of the gifts and graces of the Bible are one's own and all interpreters are servants and friends, we cannot limit the social and political ramifications.

A religion, culture or society that ignores or abuses equal rights, where the rich exploit the poor and factor large groups of people out of government and religion for any reason, a flagrant evil occurs, according to the main messages of the Bible. Will we provide a politically, socially, ethically and economically forward–looking Biblical hermeneutics in the world come of age, opposing all forms of cheap grace Liberalism and Fundamentalism, rationalism and emotivism as well as Powell?

Mosala's hermeneutic task in South Africa includes conclusions pertinent at the end of this study. He identifies three options among Africans. The first is the old Ethiopian Royalist hermeneutics based on the Royal Psalms. They seek restoration of monarchies in Ethiopia and other former monarchies. The second is the bourgeois hermeneutics familiar to readers of this book. Largely products of Christian missionary education, they are the intelligentsia (like Mosala), the official African Liberation Theologians of the 1970s and 1980s, Nobel Peace Prize winner Archbishop Desmond Tutu and Reformed Pastor–Theologian Allan Boesak (Tutu, *Hope and Suffering* and Boesak, *Farewell to Innocence*). The third consciously adopts a working–class perspective in Zion–Apostolic congregations that spring up all over Africa in search of freedom before, during and after Apartheid. He perceives the greatest potential and validity in the third option because the working–class hermeneutics, subversive and nonsystematic, favoring the struggles of members, follows a main theme of the apostles and prophets of the Bible, the scene and weapon of racial, gender and class struggles. He says the poor and exploited must free the Bible from Royalist and Middle Class captivity in order for the Bible to free them (Mosala, 191ff).

In conclusion, what I learn from Powell to move us toward the hope I share with such diverse a bunch? Many things, some still emerge. I believe, with Powell in the necessity of a philosophy of Progress for hermeneutics. By that, I do not mean previously conceived metaphysics, phenomenology or existence philosophy which closes off fresh, new discoveries. Nor do I mean some miserable circle in which to play alligators–in–the–barrel or dogs–chasing–our–tails until we harass and destroy one another, but a philosophy enabling us to read the Bible which is as much an inescapable part of us as sin.

Spirit, passion and intellectual discipline all belong to an adequate philosophy of hermeneutics that can interpret the Bible with the many scholarly and linguistic nuances of meaning flowing in the service of passions and Spirit intermingled within its pages. Doing a job of form–critical exegesis is hard work, involving detailed, scholarly analysis. Powell never short–changes people in this regard. He is a manuscript preacher and lecturer. He is never content with a sermon or lecture until there is spirit, passion and thought capable of emotionalizing people to act in agreement with God's progressive commands. The fire of God mingles with his blood, sweat and tears. Johnson says he wrestles with the text. Powell says the text wrestles with him, like Jacob and the Lord wrestling at Peniel in Genesis 32.22–32, after which his name is Israel. Cone, a spirited, passionate and intellectually rigorous interpreter, comes close to a North American post–Holocaust hermeneutics, just as the Barmen Theological Declaration provides for the Confessing Church even as Nazi–Fascist dastardly deeds take place. (Robert Osborn, *The Barmen Theological Declaration as a Paradigm for a Theology of the American Church*, 182ff, "The Black Church: The Church for the World.") The need for Biblical reflection and action in Brazil is a signpost for Claudio de Oliveira Ribeiro ("Has Liberation Theology Died?" *Ecumenical Review,* July, 1999). I carry this responsibility to illiterate and unschooled but literate preachers in my workshops because the Spirit calls preachers to form churches where hierarchical and bourgeois clergy fear to tread; I hope Mosala does the same. This is the moral responsibility of theological education. A moral phenomenology in philosophy is important. The lack of compassion in existentialism does damage to warrant more criticism by philosophers as well as theologians. The horrid fiction we live with in the U. S. is the attempt of Fundamentalists to posit theology without philosophy, most making the same mistake Tertullian makes, reducing theology to law. Can the philo–sophical downward turn of love, Scheler's *ordo amoris*, as Alves pursues, enable interpretation of the Bible?

Another philosophical presupposition I accept from Bonhoeffer's *Life Together* (91–94) and homiletic lectures at the Confessing Church seminary in Finkenwalde (Clyde Fant, *Bonhoeffer: Worldly Preaching*) that I discover he gets from Powell is emotional, mental and spiritual emptiness before coming to the Bible at all, a principle I believe he receives from Powell. The events of September 11, 2001 in Manhattan a few blocks from where I teach transform the presuppositions of Biblical interpreters. They run out of us, driven by sheer terror and we turn again to our ancestors, theologizing first and intellectually reflecting, second. The discipline of emptying ourselves of family, social and cultural concerns and conscience, I receive content from aspects of Biblical revelation that concern us (cf Osborn's proposal, 198–206). The Stoic, Hedonist and Epicurean philosophers consider human relationships in the ancient material. Historians today celebrate the Stoic Caesars of Rome for their moral political innovations including welfare programs for children, orphans, widows and the elderly in general.

Some presuppositions are important, however, because of historical terrors for which we are responsible. In the world of historical holocausts and genocides at the hands of Europeans and European-Americans, we include survivors of those atrocities only because we accept the responsibility for what our ancestors do. More people live on earth than ever before and all have distinctive voices, religions, cultures and societies whose reality we include rather than exclude because and if we learn our lesson about the necessity of ethics. The reassertion of Liberalism deflates the possibility of justice and full freedom replacing oppression for Ribeiro.

The disciplines the downward turn of love imposes on the academy as well as the church includes an exciting, thrilling outreach that includes excluded people in the spiritual and political conversation about the Biblical material, for they are the proper living subjects chosen for special consideration by the living God-subject of the Bible. The conservative role churches have now is to share our faith, about which not many of us are all that passionate anyway. How about getting together with some actual sinners to study the Bible, really hearing each other's joys and concerns? Who will pay the bills for this work?

The other hermeneutical point of philosophy Middle Class North Americans try all the time is meeting with excluded groups to organize non-violent change movements. With Cone, Leonardo Boff and Jon Sobrino, Osborn advocates criticism of our own context, asking if we are where faithful, responsible listening can even happen (Osborn, 222). Jonathan Kozol works with poor and oppressed people. In a worship service on Mother's Day in a South Bronx Church, he confronts the task of responsible listening, not as Heidegger thinks but Scheler, with a downward turn of love.

Next, we must expect and be open to surprises from the Bible and incoming people which bring new joys, justice and freedom to enlighten the dark corners of our reality. Kozol does not make sense out of anything he experiences as a suburbanite sojourning in the South Bronx. He has no answers to the questions, no solutions to the problems. He has a history of such inanities, however, which is why so many entities keep on asking him for same while disappointment's children die (Kozol, *Amazing Grace: The Lives of Children and the Conscience of a Nation*, 230, 23).

Can we base religion, culture and society on peace rather than violence? I cannot count the times I hear professional athletes and other entertainment celebrities refer to people as heroes in the wake of September 11. They receive exorbitant salaries by the controlling violent values of the power elites. The hero as defeater of enemies by violence is the leading figure at all levels of rhetoric. Is this why the religious voice always takes the form of fool, clown, criminal, villain or investigator of criminals or, in the case of current religious television, innocuous nondescript Protestant minister or still trying, with Fundamentalism, to prove details of Biblical stories, such as a floating axe–head are really just natural phenomena after all, as Harris the anti–Fundamentalist thinks?

Be suspicious of any religion or spirituality which has no actions at all to elevate the masses of poor people. Our failure in this direction is shameful. A poor woman's son calls Kozol in the middle of the night. His mother has HIV/AIDS. The conversation is theological. If God is powerful and wise enough to make trees and kidneys, why can't God stop evil and change our hearts? Recently, a woman seminarian returns from Cuba, where she talks with Sergio Arce. She asks him what he thinks of the emphasis on spirituality in the United States. Arce said, "Not much." He notes how cheap–grace Fundamentalists in the United States deprive Cuba of medicines to heal the sick. A Cuban exile regales me with all the reasons why she still gets to hate Castro immediately after hearing my evidently ineffective sermon about Jesus commanding us to love our enemies.

Be suspicious of extremists of emotion or reason. The streets in the South Bronx are named for Martin Luther King, Langston Hughes and James Weldon Johnson. The drugs everywhere are called Jungle Fever, Black Sabbath, True Power and Black Death, Kozol reports. I know, too, because I am interim minister in a Bronx church for eighteen months. Like Kozol, I see young men with their heads shaved, prison style. Why? Kozol notes people acting as though they are already in prison. (36f.) They go around with shoes sans laces in solidarity with those in prison, whose shoelaces are taken from them.

Suspect any limitations on love and equality. Ebonics is one of the racist myths. I live and work in African–American communities, and affirm, with Kozol, that most every African–American child speaks good English. We gag on gnats while swallowing camels, as Jesus says in Matthew 23.24.

Beware of Euro–centrism. Ex–President Clinton comes to Harlem. OK. What about the incoming, mainly European–Americans, displacing long–time Harlem residents? A cause James Forbes takes up, but for how long and how effectively? The Welfare Reform Act Clinton signed some years ago deprives poor people of by preparing them to work for less money than we provided for them in the old system. What happens to them in our depressed economy after September 11? We do not have enough food to supply the run on church food pantries while millions of dollars for victims of September 11 are meted out in the smallest of spoonfuls to the victims: Did we learn from the versions of Charles Dickens' *A Christmas Carol* shown on television stations?

Beware of the diatribes of resentment and retribution. One of the texts Kozol's South Bronx preacher interprets is the story of Hagar and Ishmael in Genesis 21.8–21 (Re: Ernst Knauf, "Hagar" in *Anchor Bible Dictionary*, Volume 3, 18f). Although Sarah, the free and powerful wife, sends the poor, slave wife packing, the Lord takes care of Hagar and her child. The Womanist preacher does not care what sociologists say, Hagar is a single mother. The single mothers in her church do not have men like Abraham to support them like Sarah. She assures them that God's blessing of Hagar and Ishmael means God blesses every mother and child on earth (Kozol, 227). That a preacher addresses the Hagar–Ishmael text according to the ecumenical lectionary in a rich European–American church may help them face the truth about our political economics. A couple of my Seminary friends run the Black Mountain Presbyterian Home for Children in North Carolina. They expand their operation many times larger because of the number of poor women who abandon their children to orphanages rather than keep them when there will be no safety net and no economic development increases faster than their ability to receive them. The periscope appears on the first Sunday after Trinity in Year A of the lectionary, which falls between June 19 and 25. The Psalm is 86, the epistle reading is Romans 6.1b–11 and the Gospel is Matthew 10.24–39. The psalm begs God for help in overcoming enemies out of God's eternal, steadfast love. Maybe an echo from Burroughs and Powell calls on the fathers of the single mothers' children to stop singing, "I Can't Give You Anything But Love, Baby," and get on with becoming grown–up, responsible men, husbands and fathers. Where is their steadfast love that endures forever? Paul's voice chimes right in: How can you go on living in and committing sin after you have been baptized into the death and resurrection of Jesus? The voice of Jesus cuts through all the excuses religion, culture and society make to do evil. Jesus calls us to consider sparrows. God cares for them and their chicks; will God not take care of people who have so little? Wonder why Ishmael shows up to help his brother, Isaac bury their father (Genesis 25.9?) Is Abraham God's name written on Hagar's hand?

Beware of cheap grace pity without justice. In the same sermon Kozol cites, in spite of living in Hunt's Point she rises and praises her mother and her children. In spite of oppression, bigotry and violence she thanks God for her family. In pain, we wonder how we will get the strength to go on (228). Kozol cites a thirteen–year–old boy who puts Groucho Marx glasses on, reminding Kozol he is playful and only 13, in spite of being more thoughtful because of the death and dying he experiences (239). Without preaching justice and morality, all the pity and consolation Kozol and the preacher muster are as meaningful as band–aids on gashes. We continue the struggle for political equality where the Bible, Spiritually appeals for justice higher than cheap grace philanthropy. That is what I learn about hermeneutics from Clayton Powell, 1865–1953, and how he helps the Bible interpret me so I take risks large or larger than the ones he takes when he preaches, joyfully and freely, the Gospel of Jesus Christ. More than a new psychology, or self–understanding, the horizon of the Biblical text transforms society, culture and religion, beyond Lategan (Op cit, 154, with Osborn, Op cit), which is why I bring hermeneutics into the Philosophical Hermeneutics and Moral Psychology debates. Those who take King and Gandhi seriously do not limit Moral Psychology to the personal simply because we exist in relationships. When African–American clergy threaten him with death, he responds in a way that summarizes his hermeneutics and where we may go. He assures everyone that death threats do not prevent him from sticking to his gospel guns. He thinks that if an African–American minister dies for telling the truth, their ministry will receive a boost. Perhaps his death will provoke African clergy to rise up and carry out their duty. He is willing to give his life (*Against,* 220). The death of his German Sunday School Teacher inspires us to liberating mission and, reading Powell, to a more inclusive freedom than theirs.

Select Bibliography

"Abyssinian Baptist Church," *New York Age*, December 3, 1908; March 4 and March 25, 1909.

"Abyssinian's Pastor Praises Mayor Walker," *New York Age*, December 13, 1930.

Adler, Alfred, *The Science of Living,* Garden City: Garden City Publishing Company, 1929.

—— *Superiority and Social Interest,* New York: W. W. Norton and Company, Incorporated, 1979.

Amery, Jean, *At the Mind's Limits,* New York: Schocken Books, 1986.

Aniante, Annamaria, "Papini Returns to Anarchy," *Living Age,* April, 1931.

Asante, Molefi, *The Afrocentric Idea,* Philadelphia: Temple University Press, 1987.

Bacon, Leonard, "Wild Man's Lexicon," *Saturday Review of Literature*, March 21, 1942.

Baeta, C. G., Editor., *Christianity in Tropical Africa,* New York: Oxford University Press, 1968.

Bainton, Roland H., *Yale and the Ministry,* New York: Harper and Brothers, 1957.

Barth, Karl, *Church Dogmatics,* Edinburgh: T. and T. Clark, 1936–1977.

—— *The Epistle to the Romans,* New York: Oxford University Press, 1933.

Barth, Markus, *Conversation With the Bible,* New York: Holt, Rinehart and Winston, 1964.

Bascom, John, "Faith and Philosophy," *The Dial*, August 1, 1897.

—— *Philosophy of Rhetoric*, New York: George Putnam's Sons, 1883.

—— *The Science of Mind,* New York: George P. Putnam's Sons, 1881.

—— *Things Learned By Living*, New York: George P. Putnam's Sons, 1913.

Bercovitch, Sacvan, *Puritan Origins of the American Self*, New Haven: Yale University Press, 1975.

Berger, Peter L., *Facing Up to Modernity*, New York: Harper and Row, 1977.

Bethge, Eberhard, *Dietrich Bonhoeffer: Man of Vision, Man of Courage*, New York: Harper and Row, Publishers, 1970.

Beuf, Carlo, "Portrait of Giovanni Papini," *The Saturday Review*, January 31, 1948.

Blackwell, James E., *The Black Community: Diversity and Unity*, New York: Dodd, Mead and Company, 1975.

Boesak, Allan, *Farewell to Innocence: A Social–Ethical Study of Black Theology and Black Power,* Johannesberg: Ravan, 1976.

Bonhoeffer, Dietrich, *Life Together,* New York: Harper and Row, 1954.

—— *No Rusty Swords,* New York: Harper and Row, Publishers, 1965, E. T. of the 1947 book.

Bowman, Douglas C., *Beyond the Modern Mind,* New York: Pilgrim Press, 1990.

Brooks, Lester and Parris, Guichard, *Blacks in the City, A History of the National Urban League*, Boston: Little, Brown and Company, 1971.

Callahan, Sidney Cornelia, *In Good Conscience,* San Francisco: Harper-SanFransisco, 1991.

Capeci, Dominic J., Jr., *The Harlem Riot of 1943*, Philadelphia: Temple University Press, 1977.

Chardin, Pierre Teilhard De, *The Divine Milieu: An Essay on the Interior Life*, New York: Harper and Row, 1960.

—— *Hymn of the Universe,* New York: Harper and Row, 1961.

Cheek, William F., *John Mercer Langston and the Fight for Black Freedom 1829–1865,* Urbana: The University of Illinois Press, 1989.

"Church Makes Fine Showing," *New York Age*, May 18, 1918.

Clark, Shelton, *Black Clergy as Agents of Social Change with an Emphasis on the Life of Adam Clayton Powell* [Jr.] Rutgers University Ed.D. dissertation, New Brunswick, New Jersey: Rutgers University, 1978.

Cleage, Albert, Jr., *Black Christian Nationalism*, New York: William Morrow Company, 1972.

Cobb, Howell, *A Scriptural Examination of the Institution of Slavery in The United States with its Objects and Purposes,* Atlanta: by the Author, 1856.

Cochrane, Arthur, *The Church's Confession Under Hitler,* Pittsburgh: Pickwick Press, 1976

—— *The Existentialists and God; being and the being of God in the thought of Soeren Kierkegaard, Karl Jaspers, Martin Heidegger Jean–Paul Sartre, Paul Tillich, Etienne Gilson and Karl Barth*, Philadelphia: The Westminster Press, 1956

—— *Eating and Drinking with Jesus: An Ethical and Biblical Inquiry,* Philadelphia: The Westminster Press, 1974.

Comte, Auguste, *Course of Positive Philosophy* (Six Volumes), 1830–42), Translated by Harriet Martineau, New York: C. Blanchard, 1856

—— *The Foundation of Sociology,* Edited by Kenneth Thompson, New York: Wiley, 1975

Cone, James Hal, *Black Theology and Black Power*, New York: Seabury Press, 1969.

—— and Wilmore, Gayraud, Editors, *Black Theology, a Documentary History, 2 Vols: 1966–1979, 1980–1992,* Maryknoll: Orbis Books, 1993.

—— *A Black Theology of Liberation,* Maryknoll: Orbis Books, 1987.

—— *For My People: Black Theology and the Black Church,* Maryknoll: Orbis Books, 1984.

—— *My Soul Looks Back,* Maryknoll: Orbis Books, 1986.

—— *Speaking the Truth,* Grand Rapids: Wm. B. Erdmans Publishing Company, 1986.

—— *The Spirituals and the Blues,* New York: Seabury Press, 1972.

Connors, Joseph, *Catholic Homiletic Theory in Historical Perspective,* Evanston: Northwestern University, 1962.

Conrad, Joseph, *Joseph Conrad: Selected Works,* Avenel, N.J.: Gramercy Press, 1994.

Costen, Melva Wilson, *African American Christian Worship,* Nashville: Abingdon Press, 1993.

Cox, Harvey, *Religion in the Secular City: Toward a Post Modern Theology,* New York: Simon and Schuster, 1984.

—— *The Secular City,* New York: The Macmillan Company, 1965.

Crook, David Paul, *Benjamin Kidd: Portrait of a Social Darwinian*, New York: Cambridge University Press, 1984.

Davis, Lenwood, "Frederick Douglass as an A. M. E. Zion Preacher," *The A. M. E. Zion Quarterly Review*, October, 1996.

Dickens, Charles, *A Christmas Carol,* Television and Cinema Versions, 2001

Dostoyevsky, Fyodor, *The Brothers Karamasov,* New York: E. P. Dutton, 1936

—— *The Idiot,* Translated by David Magarshack, New York: Penguin Books, 1955

Douglass, Frederick, *My Bondage and My Freedom*, New York: Miller, Orton and Mulligan, 1855.

—— *The Frederick Douglass Papers,* New Haven: Yale University Press, 1979.

"Dr. A. C. Powell Starts Drive Among Abyssinian Church Members to Relieve the Unemployment Situation," *The New York Age*, December 6, 1930.

"Dr. Powell Calls on Church to Recapture Social Leadership Lost to Politicians," *New York Times*, November 10, 1940.

Durant, William J., *Philosophy and the Social Problem,* New York: Macmillan, 1917.

—— *Socialism and Anarchism,* New York: Albert and Charles Boni, 1914.

—— *The Story of Philosophy,* New York: Simon and Schuster, 1926, 1961.

Epp, Eldon Jay and MacRae, George W., Editors, *The New Testament and its Modern Interpreters* Atlanta: Scholars Press, 1989.

Fant, Cylde, *Bonhoeffer: Worldly Preaching,* Nashville: Thomas Nelson, 1975.

Farias, Victor, *Heidegger and Nazism*, Philadelphia: Temple University Press, 1987.

Ferm, William, Editor, *Third World Liberation Theologies: A Reader,* Maryknoll: Orbis Books, 1986.

Fisher, Miles Mark, Editor, *Virginia Union University and Some of Her Achievements, 25th Anniversary, 1899–1924,* Richmond: Brown Print Shop, 1924.

Flew, Antony, Editor, *Dictionary of Philosophy*, Revised Second Edition, New York: St. Martin's Press, 1979.

Foner, Philip, Editor, *The Black Panthers Speak*, New York: J. B. Lippincott Company, 1970

—— Editor, *Frederick Douglass on Women's Rights,* Westport, Conn.: Greenwood Press, 1955.

—— Editor, *The Life and Writings of Frederick Douglass, the Early Years,* New York: International Publishers, 1950.

—— Editor, *The Voice of Black America,* New York: Simon and Schuster, 1972.

Frackenheim, Emil, *To Mend the World*, New York: Schocken Books, 1989.

Franklin, John Hope, *From Slavery to Freedom, A History of Negro Americans,* New York: Vintage Books, 1969.

Freedman, David, Editor, *The Anchor Bible Dictionary,* New York: Doubleday, 1992.

Frei, Hans, *The Eclipse of Biblical Narrative: A Study in Eighteenth and Nineteenth Century Hermeneutics,* New Haven: Yale University Press, 1974.

Frey, Raymond, *William James Durant: An Intellectual Biography,* Lewiston, New York: The Edwin Mellin Press, 1991.

Frings, Manfred, Editor, *Max Scheler (1874–1928) Centennial Essays,* The Hague: Martin and Nijhoff, 1974.

Frings, Manfred, *Max Scheler, A Concise Introduction to the World of a Great Thinker,* Pittsburgh: Duquesne University Press, 1965.

Gatewood, W. B., *Aristocrats of Color: the Black Elite, 1880–1920,* Bloomington: Indiana University Press, 1990.

Gollwitzer, Helmut, *The Demands of Freedom,* London: SCM Press, 1965.

Gonzalez, Justo and Catherine, *Liberation Preaching: The Pulpit and the Oppressed,* Nashville: Abingdon Press, 1980.

Greenberg, Cheryl Lynn, *"Or Does It Explode?" Black Harlem in the Great Depression,* New York: Oxford University Press, 1991.

Gruenler, Royce Gordon, *Meaning and Understanding: The Philosophical Framework for Biblical Interpretation,* Grand Rapids: Zondervan Publishing House, 1991.

Guardini, Igino, "Croce and Papini," *Commonweal,* August 3, 1932.

Hamilton, Charles V., *Adam Clayton Powell, Jr.: The Political Biography of an American Dilemma,* New York: Macmillan Publishing Company, 1991.

Harris, Samuel J., *God: Creator and Lord of All, Vol.1,* New York: Charles Scribner's Sons, 1896.

—— *God Our Savior,* New Haven: Yale Divinity School Library, an unpublished, 795–page manuscript dated August 19, 1896.

—— *The Philosophical Basis of Theism,* New York: Charles Scribner's Sons, 1898.

—— *The Self-Revelation of God,* New York: George P. Putnam's Sons, 1887.

—— *The Kingdom of Christ on Earth: Twelve Lectures,* Andover: W. F. Draper, 1874.

Hartshorn, W. N. and Penniman, George W., Editors, *An Era of Progress And Promise, 1863–1910,* Boston: Priscilla Publishing Company, 1910.

Hatch, Nathan and Noll, Mark, Editors, *The Bible in America: Essays in Cultural History,* New York: Oxford University Press, 1982.

Heaps, Willard A., *Riots U. S. A., 1765–1970,* New York: Seabury Press, 1970.

Higginbotham, Evelyn Brooks, *Righteous Discontent: The Women's Movement in the Black Baptist Church,* Cambridge, MA: Harvard University Press, 1993.

Hirsch, David H., *The Deconstruction of Literature: Criticism After Auschwitz,* Hanover, NH: The University Press of New England, 1991.

Hogan, Patrick Colm, *The Politics of Deconstruction: Ideology, Professionalism and the Study of Literature,* New York: Oxford University Press, 1990.

Holland, Scott, "First We Take Manhattan, Then on to Berlin: Dietrich Bonhoeffer's New York," *CrossCurrents,* New Rochelle, New York, Autumn, 2001.

Holloway, William M., Editor, *Whither the Negro Church?* New Haven: City Printing Company, 1931.

Hood, James W., *One Hundred Years of the African Episcopal Methodist Zion Church,* New York: A. M. E. Zion Book Concern, 1895.

Jackson, Leonard, *The Poverty of Structuralism: Literature and Structuralist Theory,* New York: Longman Group UK Limited, 1991.

Johnson, Joseph A., Jr., *Proclamation Theology,* Shreveport: The Fourth Episcopal District Press, 1977.

Kaesemann, Ernst, *Jesus Means Freedom,* London: SCM Press, 1969.

Kelly, Eugene, *Max Scheler,* Boston: Twayne Publishers, 1977.

Kelly, Geffrey and Nelson, Burton, Editors, *A Testament to Freedom: The Essential Writings of Dietrich Bonhoeffer,* San Francisco: HarperSanFrancisco, 1990.

Kelly, Michael, Editor, *Critique and Power: Recasting the Foucault/ Habermas Debate,* Cambridge, MA: The Massachusetts Institute of Technology Press, 1994.

Kidd, Benjamin, *Social Evolution,* New York: George P. Putnam's Sons, 1892, Revision of 1921.

Kidd, Benjamin, *The Science of Power,* New York: George P. Putnam's Sons, 1918.

King, George M. P., *The Baptist Home Mission Monthly,* The American Baptist Convention, April, 1880; June, 1880; March, 1885; March, 1887.

King, Martin Luther, Jr., *The Conceptions of God in the Theologies of Henry Nelson Weiman and Paul Tillich,* Boston University Ph.D., 1955, Ann Arbor: University Microfilms, Inc., 1955.

Kinney, John W., *Adam Clayton Powell, Sr. and Adam Clayton Powell, Jr.: A Historical Exposition and Theological Analysis,* Columbia University Ph.D., Ann Arbor: University Microfilms, 1979.

Knauf, Ernst, "Hagar," D. N. Freedman, Editor, *The Anchor Bible Dictionary,* Volume 3, New York: Doubleday, 1992

Kozol, Jonathan, *Amazing Grace: The Lives of Children and the Cons- Conscience of a Nation,* New York: Crown Publishers, 1995.

Lambert, Richard D., Editor, *Religion in American Society–American Academy of Political and Social Sciences*, November, 1960.

Lewis, David L., *When Harlem was in Vogue*, New York: Oxford University Press, 1979.

Lincoln, C. Eric and Maniya, Lawrence H., Editors, *The Black Church in The African American Experience,* Durham: Duke University Press, 1990, and Maryknoll: Orbis Press, 1993.

Logan, Rayford and Winston, Michael, Editors, *Dictionary of American Negro Biography,* New York: Norton and Company, 1982.

Logan, Rayford, *The Negro in the U. S., Vol. 1: History to 1945–From Slavery to Second Class Citizenship,* New York: Van Norstrand, Reinhold and Company, 1970.

Low, W. Augustus, Editor, *Encyclopedia of Black America,* New York: McGraw–Hill Book Company, 1951.

Lynch, John R., *The Facts of Reconstruction*, New York: Arno Press, 1968.

_____, *Reminiscences of an Active Life*, Chicago: The University of Chicago Press, 1968.

The Making of Black America, Vol.1, The Origins of Black Americans New York: Athenum, 1969.

Maranza, C., "Papini: Warrior at Rest," *The Catholic World,* October, 1957.

Maritain, Raissa, *Leon Bloy, Pilgrim of the Absolute,* London: Eyre and Spottiswoods, 1947.

Mazza, Maria Serafina, "Giovanni Papini's Threescore Years–and–Ten," *Catholic World*, September,1951.

"Meekness Held Negroes' Salvation," *New York Times*, November 14, 1943.

Meier, August, *Negro Thought in America, 1880–1915, Part V*, Ann Arbor: University of Michigan Press, 1963.

Mencken, Henry L., "The Afraamerican: New Style," *The American Mercury*, February, 1926.

—— "The Burden of Credulity," *Opportunity: A Journal of Negro Life*, February, 1931.

—— "Dunghill Varieties of Christianity," *Opportunity*, February, 1931.

Miller, Kelly, *Radicals and Conservatives and Other Essays on the Negro in America,* New York: Schocken Books, 1968.

"Ministers and Businessmen," *New York Age*, August 21, 1916.

"Minister Calls Mass Meeting," *New York Age*, June 8, 1911.

Mosala, Itumeleg J., *Biblical Hermeneutics and Black Theology in South Africa,* Grand Rapids: Wm. B. Eerdmans, 1989.

Mueller–Vollmer, Kurt, Editor, *The Hermeneutics Reader, Texts of the German Tradition from the Enlightenment to the Present,* New York: The Continuum Press, 1994.

Murtchison, Carl, Editor, *Psychologies of 1930,* Worcester, MA.: Clark University Press, 1930.

Murray, Albert, *The Omni–American*, New York: Vintage Press, 1970.

"Negro Baptists to March on Washington," *New York Age*, September 21, 1911.

Nelson, John A., "Christ in Popular Literature," *Catholic World*, includes review of *Life of Christ*, August, 1929.

Oakley, Justin, *Morality and the Emotions*, New York: Routledge, 1992.

Oakley, Keith, *Best Laid Schemes: The Psychology of Emotions*, New York: Cambridge University Press, 1992.

Oglesby, Enoch H., *Ethics and Theology From the Other Side: Sounds of Moral Struggle,* New York: University Press of America, 1979.

Osborn, Robert T., *The Barmen Theological Declaration as a Paradigm for a Theology of the American Church,* Toronto: The Edwin Mellen Press, 1991.

Ottley, Roi and Weatherby, William, Jr., Editors, *The Negro in New York: An Informal Social History,* New York: The New York Public Library, 1967.

Papini, Giovanni, *Saint Augustine,* New York: Harcourt, Brace and Company, 1930.

—— *The Devil,* New York: E. P. Dutton, 1953.

—— *The Letters of Pope Celestine VI to All Mankind,* New York: E.P Dutton and Co., 1948.

—— *The Life of Christ,* New York: Harcourt, Brace and Company, 1927.

Peck, George Wilbur, *Peck's Bad Boy and His Pa and Compendium of Fun,* Cutchogue, NY: Buccaneer Books, Inc., 1976

Powell, Adam Clayton Powell, Jr., *Adam By Adam,* New York: Dial Press, 1971.

Powell, Adam Clayton Powell, Sr., *Against the Tide,* New York: Richard R. Smith, 1938 and Salem, New Hampshire: Ayer, 1992.

—— "A Graceless Church," *New York Age,* September 21, 1911.

—— "American Religion is an Abomination with God," *The New York Age,* May 14, 1914.

—— "A Model Church," *The Watchman–Examiner, a National Baptist Paper,* November 27, 1930.

—— *A Souvenir of the Immanuel Baptist Church and its Members,* New Haven: Clarence H. Ryder, 1895.

—— "The Bible is More Than Literature," *Negro Pulpit Opinion*, March, 1927.

—— "The Church in Social Work," *Opportunity: A Journal of Negro Life*, National Urban League, Vol.1, January, 1923.

—— "Give Me That Old Time Religion," *Negro Digest*, May, 1950.

—— "H. L. Mencken Finds Flowers in a Dunghill," *Opportunity: A Journal of Negro Life*, 1931.

—— "The Negro's Enrichment of the Church Today," *The Watchman–Examiner*, July 22, 1937.

—— *Palestine and Saints in Caesar's Household*, New York: Richard R. Smith, 1939.

—— *Patriotism and the Negro,* New York: Beehive Publishing, 1918.

—— *Picketing Hell*, New York: Wendell Malliet, 1942.

—— "Progress–The Law of Life," *Negro Pulpit Opinion,* January 15, 1928.

—— "The Religion of Frederick Douglass," *The Colored American*, April, 1902.

—— *Riots and Ruins,* New York: Richard R. Smith, 1945.

—— "Rocking the Gospel Train," *Negro Digest*, April, 1951.

—— "The Silent Church," *The Amsterdam News*, February, 1935.

—— "Tolerance in Race and Religion," *The Watchman–Examiner*, 1941.

—— *Upon This Rock*, New York: Abyssinian Baptist Church, 1949.

Pugh, Roderick W., *Psychology and the Black Experience,* Monterey, California: Brooks/Cole Publishing Company, 1972.

Putnam, Samuel, "A Letter From Italy," *Saturday Review of Literature*, February 15, 1930.

Raboteau, Alfred J., *Slave Religion: The "Invisible Institution" in the Antebellum South,* New York: Oxford University Press, 1978.

Ranly, Ernest W., *Scheler's Phenomenology of Community*, The Hague: Martinus Nijhoff, 1966.

Raybould, A. N., "In the Vanguard of Catholic Thought," *Catholic World*, from Papini's *Pilota Cieco*, September, 1933.

Reviews of Papini's *The Devil*, *Newsweek*, November 4, 1954, and *Time*, January 4, 1954.

Review of Harris's *God*, *Catholic World*, January, 1897.

Review of Harris's *God*, *The Outlook*, February 26, 1898.

Ribeiro, Claudio de Oliveira, "Has Liberation Theology Died?" *Ecumenical Review*, Bossey, Switzerland: The World Council of Churches, July, 1999.

Ricoeur, Paul, *From Text to Action, Essays in Hermeneutics, II*, Evanston: Northwestern University Press, 1986.

Robinson, Sanford, *John Bascom, Prophet*, New York: G. P. Putnam's Sons, 1922.

Sandeen, Ernest, Editor, *The Bible and Social Reform,* Philadelphia: Fortress Press; Chico, California: Scholars Press, 1982.

Shannon, David and Wilmore, Gayraud, Editors, *Black Witness to the Apostolic Faith*, Grand Rapids: Wm B. Eerdmans Publishing Company, 1988.

Scheimer, Seth, *Negro Mecca: A History of the Negro in New York City 1865–1920*, New York: New York University Press, 1965.

Scheler, Max, *The Genius of War and the German War,* Leipzig, 1915

Shannon, David, *The Old Testament Experience of Faith,* Valley Forge: Judson Press, 1977.

Silverman, Hugo, Editor, *Gadamer and Hermeneutics*, New York: Routledge, Chapman and Hall, Inc., 1991.

Simonson, Rick and Walker, Scott, Editors, *The Graywolf Annual Five: Multi-Cultural Literacy.* Saint Paul: Graywolf Press, 1988.

Sloan, Irving, *Our Violent Past: An American Chronicle,* New York: Random House, 1970.

Sontag, Frederick and Roth, John K., *The American Religious Experience,* New York: Harper and Row, 1972.

Taggart, Sarah R., *Living as If: Belief Systems in Mental Health Practice,* San Francisco: Jossey-Bass Publishers, 1994.

"Tells Negroes to Wage Bloodless War," *New York Age*, March 29, 1917.

"The World's Richest Baptist Church," *New York Age*, April 17, 1913.

Tolstoy, Leo, *War and Peace,* Maude Translation, Edited by George Gibian, New York: W. W. Norton, 1966

Tutu, Desmond, *Hope and Suffering,* Grand Rapids: Eerdmans, 1984.

Virginia Union Bulletin Centennial Issue: A Century of Service to Education and Religion, 1865-1965, Richmond: Virginia Union University, June, 1965.

Wallace, Jay, *Responsibility and the Moral Sentiments*, Cambridge, MA: Harvard University Press, 1994.

Warner, Robert Austin, *New Haven Negroes: A Social History,* New Haven: Yale University Press, 1940.

Washington, James Melvin, *Frustrated Fellowship: The Black Baptist Quest for Social Power,* Macon, Georgia: The Mercer University Press, 1986.

Washington, Joseph R., Jr., *Black Religion: The Negro and Christianity in the United States,* Boston: Beacon Press, 1964.

Weiss, Nancy J., *The National Urban League, 1910–1940,* New York: Oxford University Press, 1974.

Weld, Theodore Dwight, *The Bible Against Slavery,* New York: Anti-Slavery Society, Fourth Edition, 1938.

Welty, William, *Black Shepherds: A Study of the Leading Negro Clergymen in New York City, 1900–1940,* New York University Ph.D., 1969.

White, Ronald Cedric, Jr., *Social Christianity and the Negro in the Progressive Era, 1890–1920,* Princeton University Ph.D., 1972, Ann Arbor: University Microfilms, 1972.

Whittaker, Frederick W., *Samuel Harris, American Theologian,* New York: Vantage Press, 1982.

Wimberly, Edward P., *Pastoral Care in the Black Church,* Nashville: Abingdon Press, 1979.

—— *Pastoral Counseling and Spiritual Values: A Black Point of View,* Nashville: Abingdon Press, 1982.

Wind, Renate, *A Spoke in the Wheel: Dietrich Bonhoeffer,* translated by John Bowden, Grand Rapids: Eerdmans, 1990

Wise, Carroll A., *Psychiatry and the Bible,* New York: Harper and Brothers, 1956.

Young, Josiah Ulysses, III, *No Difference in the Fare: Dietrich Bonhoeffer and the Problem of Racism,* Grand Rapids: Eerdmans, 1998.

Zerner, Ruth, "Dietrich Bonhoeffer's American Experiences: People, Letters and Papers from Union Seminary," *The Union Seminary Quarterly Review,* Volume XXXI, Number 4, New York: Union Theological Seminary, Summer, 1976.

Zimmermann, Wolf–Dieter, *I Knew Dietrich Bonhoeffer,* edited by W–D. Zimmermann and Ronald Gregor Smith, translated by Kathe Gregor Smith, New York: Harper and Row, 1967

Scripture Index

Genesis
1–2 ... 1
3 ... 45
19 ... 45
21.8–21 ... 92
22.1–14 ... 14
25.9 ... 93
32.22–32 ... 89

Exodus
1.8–14 ... 85
14.15 ... 69
21.34 ... 58

Deuteronomy
18.15–22 ... 7

Joshua
1.6f ... 68f
9.18 ... 68f

1 Samuel
2.32 ... 66
3.11fff ... 66
4.19f ... 66

15.22 ... 14

2 Kings
2.11 ... 13

Job
2.9 ... 44,
42.10–16 ... 15

Psalm
86 ... 92
127.1 ... 30

Song of Solomon
1.5f ... 78

Isaiah
2.4 ... 13
61 ... 58

Jeremiah
31.22 ... 47

Ezekiel
34 ... 66

Amos ... 84
6.1 ... 69

Micah
6.8 ... 13

Matthew
2 ... 57
4.16 ... 57
5 ... 54, 76
5.3 ... 73
5.9f, 21–26, 43–48 ... 73
5–7 ... vi, 2, 54, 57, 79
5.38–42 ... 58
6.23 ... 57
6.24 ... 58
7.7 ... 77
7.24f ... 53
8.10–13 ... 58
8.12 ... 57
9.2–22, 29 ... 58
10.24–39 ... 92
13.22 ... 58
15.28 ... 58
19.22 ... 56
21.21ff ... 58
22.1–14 ... 53
22.13 ... 57
22.15–22 ... 59
22.34–40 ... 18
22.39 ... 20
23.24 ... 91
25 ... 66
25.30 ... 57
25.31–46 ... 59
25.34ff ... 28
26.4 ... 56
27.45 ... 57
28.18 ... 47

Mark

5.30 ... 52
6.34 ... 52
10.23 ... 58
12.13–17 ... 59
14.10–18 ... 56f
14.71 ... 52

Luke
4 ... 58
6.28 ... 13
6.29f ... 58
6.38 ... 48
9.24 ... 48
10.25–37 ... 2
10.29–37 ... 56
10.39, 42 ... 58
14.16–24 ... 53
16.8–11, 19–31 ... 58f
19.41 ... 52
20.20–26 ... 59

John ... 66
1 ... 20
1.3f, 12f, 33 ... 73
1.12f, 29 ... 13
1.35 ... 59
2.15 ... 52
4.7–28 ... 58
16.33 ... 64
17 ... 18, 53, 55
17.23 ... 53

Acts ... 65, 70
3 ... 73
4.23–35 ... 53
17.26 ... 20

Romans
6.1b–11 ... 92
14.7ff ... 27
14.10ff ... 13

1 Corinthians
13 ... 2

Galatians
2.12 ... 75
3.28 ... 12
5 ... 2

Philippians
2.12 ... 66

Colossians
3.11 ... 12

1 Thessalonians
4.11 ... 81

2 Thessalonians
3.10 ... 81

2 Timothy
3.14–17 ... 21

Philemon
15f ... 80

Hebrews
10.1–18 ... 14

James
1.26f ... 3

1 Peter
1.2–9, 13ff ... 28
2.1–5, 9–17 ... 28
2.21–25 ... 33
3.13–18, 21f ... 28
4.1–19, 5.2–11 ... 28

1 John
3.11 ... 14
5.3–5 ... 64

Names Index

Abelard, Peter, 80
Abbott, Lyman, 31
Adler, Alfred, 10, 32
Alexander the Great, 60
Allende, Salvador, 80
Allport, Gordon, 32
Alves, Rubem, 79, 81, 83f, 89
Alyosha, 15
Ambrose of Milan, 59, 81
Amery, Jean, 87
Aniante, Annamaria,
Apel, Karl–Otto, 84
Aquinas, Thomas, 58, 80
Arce–Martinez, Sergio, 91
Aristotle, 10, 16, 38, 56, 60, 84
Asante, Molefi, 5, 14f, 47, 55f, 74, 85
Augustine of Hippo, 42, 56, 81
Austin, Robert, 23

Baab, Otto, 32, 36
Bacon, Francis, 25
Bacon, Leonard, 57, 81
Bainton, Roland, 18, 43
Baldwin, James, 86

Barth, Karl, 8f, 11, 20, 27, 46f, 55, 61, 70, 72, 74f, 78, 81, 87
Barth, Marcus, 22, 29, 46, 56
Bascom, John, 26f, 37, 40f, 77f
Bayne, Laura, xviii
Beecher, Henry, 17, 40
Beecher, Lyman, 17
Benan, Jehill, 2
Bengel, Johann, 19
Bennett, Robert, 28f
Bercovitch, Sacvan, 5, 17, 19, 30, 75f, 78
Berger, Peter L., 9
Bergson, Henri, 79
Bethge, Eberhard, xi, 82
Blackwell, James, 31
Bloy, Leon, 37, 85f
Boesak, Allan, 61, 88
Boff, Leonardo, 90
Bonaparte, Napoleon, 59
Bonhoeffer, Dietrich, ix, xiff, xvii, xxf, 2ff, 5, 7, 9, 11, 14f, 23, 25, 39, 43, 47, 51, 61, 64, 66, 74ff, 82, 86, 89, 93
Bonhoeffer, Karl–Friedrich, 82

Bowles, Addie, xv
Bowles, Jake, xv
Bowman, Douglas, 9
Brown v. Topeka, Kansas School Board, 29
Brown, John, xiii, 1
Browning, Robert, 5
Bruce, Blanche, xvi, 3f
Buber, Martin, 47, 85f
Buddha, Gautama, 51
Bultmann, Rudolf, 8, 11, 33, 47, 55, 78, 87
Burroughs, Nannie H., x, xviii, 28f, 32, 74, 92
Butts, Calvin, xiii

Callahan, Sidney C., 71f, 87
Calvin, John, 80
Capeci, Dominic J., 79
Chardin, Teilhard de, 5, 8, 33, 78f
Charles I, 60
Cheek, William F., 4
Christiansen, Carl, 32
Cicero, 56
Clark, Shelton, 5f, 9, 74
Cleage, Albert, 32
Cleveland, Grover, xvi
Clingan, Maria, xxii
Clingan, R. G., ix–xiii, 1f, 4f, 7–15, 18f, 21f, 27f, 31, 33, 43, 45ff, 49–61, 64, 67f, 70–93
Clinton, William J., 92
Cobb, Howell, 22
Cochrane, Arthur, 6, 9, 55, 87
Coleridge, Samuel, 17, 20, 30f
Comte, Auguste, ix, 6, 10, 21, 30, 35f, 39f,
Cone, James, 2f, 7f, 11, 19, 29–32, 35, 63, 73, 78, 90, 92
Connors, Joseph, 56

Conrad, Joseph, 37, 41
Coogan, Jackie, 1
Costen, Melva, 5, 8f, 19f, 30, 68, 70, 73, 87
Cox, Harvey, 9, 69
Croce, Benedetto, 6, 50
Cromwell, Oliver, 60
Crook, David, 35, 39, 79
Cullen, Countee, v, 45

Dante, 56, 59
Darwin, Charles, 6, 22, 26f, 30, 36–39, 57, 59, 61, 67, 78f
Davis, Lenwood, 3
Derrida, Jacques, 56, 83
Dewey, John, x, 6–8, 26, 30, 36, 67
Dickens, Charles, 41, 92
Dilthey, W., 46f, 83, 87
Dionysius, 45
Dodd, Charles H., 46f
Dostoyevsky, F., 15, 50, 52, 77
Douglass, Frederick, x, xvii, 1–5, 7–13, 15, 23, 31f, 35, 38f, 41, 43, 56, 59, 63–65, 67–70, 74ff, 82
DuBois, W. E. B., xvii, 5, 9, 12f, 26, 31, 38, 43, 61
Durant, William, viii, 4f, 6, 14, 67ff, 71, 79–82, 83

Edwards, Jonathan, 17, 83
Epp, Eldon J., 83
Eusebius, 72
Evans, William, 22

Fant, Clyde, 89
Farias, Victor, 81
Ferm, William, 55f, 77
Ferris, William, ix, xiff, xvi, 19 49f, 87

Fisher, Frank, ix, xi, 2
Flew, Antony, 83
Foner, Philip, 2, 84
Forbes, James, 92
Foucault, Michel, 83, 85
Frackenheim, Emil, 87
Franklin, John H.,
Freeman, David N., 66
Frei, Hans, 19
Freud, Sigmund, 9, 11, 79
Frey, Raymond, 67
Frings, Manfred, 45f, 60
Fuchs, Ernst, 9, 29
Fuller, Reginald, 83

Gadamer, Hans–Georg, 86f
Gandhi, Mohandas, vii, 5, 54, 68, 69, 76, 81, 87, 93
Garrison, William L., xvii, 1, 23
Garvey, Marcus, xiv, 5, 12, 25, 32, 38
Gassett y Ortega, Jose, 46
Gatewood, W. B., 4, 12
George, David, 63
Gerzon, Mark, 11
Gladden, Washington, 31
Godwin, 59
Gollwitzer, Helmut, 60f,
Gonzalez, Catherine, 70
Gonzalez, Justo, 70
Grant, Jacqueline, 2, 77
Gray, James, 22
Greenberg, Cheryl L., 28
Gruenler, Royce G., 83
Gutierrez, G., 11, 78, 82

Habermas, Juergen, 83
Hamilton, Charles V., 5, 9, 11, 74, 77
Harris, Samuel J., x, xii, xvi, 4ff, 8ff, 13, 17–30, 32, 35, 37, 39, 42, 47, 49, 53f, 59ff, 67, 71, 75f, 77–84
Hatch, Nathan, 22f, 30
Hegel, G. F., 29, 33, 42, 46, 50, 56, 84
Heidegger, Martin, 33, 38, 40, 45ff, 54, 58, 61, 78, 81f, 83, 85ff, 91
Hello, Ernest, 37, 85
Herder, J. H. von, 46
Hickok, Laurens, 27
Higginbotham, E. B., 4
Hill, Horatio, xixf
Hirsch, David R., 84–87
Hitler, A., xvii, 33, 41, 46, 54, 66, 87
Hogan, Patrick C., 83f
Holland, Scott, viii
Holloway, William M.
Homer, 45
Hood, James W., 3
Hoover, Herbert, xvi
Houston, D. B., vi, xi
Hughes, Langston, 91
Hume, David, 71
Husserl, Edmund, 33, 45f, 48

Jackson, Andrew, 86
Jackson, Leonard, 86f
James, Thomas, 2
James, William, 26, 31, 79
Jaspers, Karl, 47
Johnson, Joseph A., 5, 8f, 11, 29ff, 69f, 78, 89
Johnson, J. W., 91
Jones, Stanley, 35
Jung, Carl G., 10, 32, 79
Juengel, Eberhard, 55

Kaesemann, Ernst, 29, 71ff
Kant, Immanuel, 6, 26, 30

Kelly, Geffrey, 66
Kelly, Michael, 83
Khan, Genghis, 59
Kidd, Benjamin, xiif, 4, 6f, 9f, 13, 22, 26–28, 35–45, 47, 49, 51, 53, 59f, 64f, 67, 74, 77–82
Kierkegaard, Soren, 33, 46, 56, 86
King, George M. P., xvi, 3f, 5, 24, 35, 38f, 59
King, Martin, Jr., xiii, 26, 87, 91, 93
Kinney, John W., 5f, 8ff, 74
Knauf, Ernst, 104
Korper, Phyllis, xiii
Kozol, Jonathan, 90–93
Kropotkin, Peter, 59, 84
Kung, Hans, 55

Lagree, Simon, 17, 41, 78, 83
Lambert, Richard D., 77
Langston, John, xv, 3f, 8, 10, 12, 38
Lasserre, Jean, 13
Lategan, Bernard, 84, 93
Lehmann, Marion, v
Lehmann, Paul, ix, xi
Lemus, Rienzi, viii, 27, 35
Lessing, Gotthold, 24
Liele, George, 63
Lincoln, Abraham, 17
Lincoln, C. Eric, 74
Link, Henry, 13
Logan, Rayford, xvii
Longfellow, Henry, 18
Low, W. Augustus, xxi
Luther, Martin, 19, 31
Lynch, John R., xi, 3f

Macquarrie, John, 8, 61

MacRae, George W., 83
Maningo, L., 74
Mankiller, Wilma, 86
Maranza, C., 49
Marcel, Gabriel, 47
Maritain, Jacques, 47, 85
Maritain, Raissa Oumansoff, 37, 86
Marx, Groucho, 93
Marx, Karl, 36, 53, 57, 61, 85
Mather, Cotton, 17f, 30
Mazza, Maria S., 49ff
Means, Inez, xxi
Meier, August, 70
Mencken, H. L., xvi, 10, 12, 21, 27, 39, 45, 52
Mill, John S., 30
Miller, Kelly, 83f
Mitchell, Mozella, xiii
Moltmann, J., 83
Mosala, Itumeleg, 8, 10, 76, 88f
Mueller–Vollmer, Kurt, 84
Murtchison, Carl, 32
Murray, Albert, 14
Mussolini, B., 49, 54f

Nelson, Burton, 66
Niebuhr, Reinhold, v, 8, 55
Nietzsche, F., 12, 33, 38, 52, 80
Noll, Mark, 22, 30

Oakley, Justin, 71
Oakley, Keith, 87f
Oglesby, Enoch H., 35
Origen, 55
Osborn, Robert T., 89f
Osiris, 58
Ottley, Roi, 82
Overbeck, F., 72f
Overstreet, Barbara, 32

Pannenberg, Wolfhart, 83
Papini, Giovanni, viii, 4, 6, 10, 13, 37, 42, 49–61, 67, 76f, 79–82, 84
Paris, Peter, 11, 13, 16
Parmenides, 45, 78
Parry, J. H., 61
Pascal, Blaise, 24, 59, 64
Pavlovic, Jacqueline, xiii
Peck, George W., xv, 1, 6
Philip of Macedonia, 60
Pinchback, Governor, xvi, 3f
Plato, 11, 60
Porter, Isaac N., xvi, 6f
Powell, Adam Clayton, Jr., xvii–xx, 4f, 36, 41, 45, 71, 86
Powell, A. Clayton, Sr., ix–xiii, xv–xxii, 1–61, 63–83, 85, 88f, 92f
Powell, Anthony, xv
Powell, Blanche, xvii, xix
Powell, Clarence, 43
Powell, Sally Dunning, xv
Proctor, Samuel D., xxii
Proudhon, 59
Pugh, Roderick, 78
Putnam, Samuel, 49

Raboteau, Alfred J., 6, 17, 20, 23, 27, 51, 63
Rauschenbusch, Walter, 31, 79
Renan, Pierre, 37, 79
Revills, Senator, xvi, 3f
Rhodes, Cecil, 7, 39
Ribeiro, Claudio, 89f
Ricoeur, Paul, 84f, 87
Robinson, Sanford, 27
Roosevelt, F. D., xvi, 78
Roosevelt, Theodore, xx, 78
Roth, John K., 18
Roethe, Richard, 26f, 37, 40

Rouault, Georges, 85
Rousseau, Jean–J., 21, 24, 42, 51, 57
Royce, Josiah, 6
Rudwick, Elliott, 12, 74
Rush, Christopher, 2
Russell, B., 6, 57, 67f

Sandeen, Ernest, 11
Sartre, Jean–P., 54f, 85
Saunders, Ernest., 32
Sawicki, Jana, 83
Schaeffer, Mattie F., xvf
Scheimer, Seth, xviii
Scheler, Max, 33, 38, 45ff, 60f, 77, 80f, 85, 89f
Schleiermacher, Albrecht, 84
Schoemann, Ferdinand, 87
Scott, Dred, 23
Segundo, Juan Luis, 11, 77f, 82
Serrington, William, 2
Shakespeare, William, xvi
Shannon, David, 8, 10, 19, 64
Silverman, Hugo, 86
Simonson, Rick, 86
Smith, Timothy, 77
Sobrino, Jon, 90
Soelle, Dorothee, 83
Sontag, Frederick, 18
Spencer, Henry, 36
Stalin, J., 54
Stirner, 59
Stowe, Harriet, 17f, 41
Straton, J., 22
Strauss, Henry, 37, 79
Strawson, Peter F., 85, 87
Strong, Josiah, 31

Taggart, Sarah R., 32
Tertullian, 89
Tillich, Paul, 8, 29, 40, 55, 61

Tolstoy, Leo, 50, 52, 77
Torrey, Reuben, 22
Tourgee, Albion, 31
Truth, Sojourner, 23
Tung, Mao Tse, 35, 39
Tuppins, Mayor, xv
Tutu, Desmond, 88

Vandlandingham, A. M. R., xx
Viviano, Pauline, 66

Walker, Scott, 86
Walker, Jimmy, 49
Wallace, Jay, 85, 87
Wallace, Michele, 86
Warner, Robert A., 65
Washington, Booker T., xvi, 4, 9, 12f, 43, 63, 71
Washington, Joseph R., Jr., 31f, 35
Watson, Gary, 87, 90
Weatherby, William, Jr., 82
Weber, Max, 84, 87
Weber, Timothy, 21f
Weems, Renita, 8, 10, 72, 77

Weiman, Henry, 30
Weld, Theodore D., 22
Welty, William, 9, 11, 64, 74
Wesley, John, 73
White, Ronald C., Jr., 36
Whittaker, Frederick W., 19–21
Wilhelm, Kaiser, 44
Williams, Delores, 77
Wilmore, Gayraud, 2, 11, 13, 19, 29, 63f
Wimberly, Edward P., 32
Winbush, Vincent, 8, 10, 82
Wind, Renate, ix, xii, 4, 9, 76
Winston, Michael, xxi
Wise, Carroll A., 31f
Wood, M. Virginia, x, 12, 74
Woodard, Tino, xiii

Young, Josiah U., xii, 4, 9, 76

Zarathustra, 58
Zerner, Ruth, ix, xii, 4, 9, 15, 76
Zimmerman, Wolf–Dieter, 15

Martin Luther King, Jr. Memorial Studies in Religion, Culture, and Social Development

Mozella G. Mitchell, General Editor

This series is named for Martin Luther King Jr., because of his superb scholarship and eminence in religion and society, and is designed to promote excellence in scholarly research and writing in areas that reflect the interrelatedness of religion and social/cultural/political development both in American society and in the world. Examination of and elaboration on religion and sociocultural components such as race relations, economic developments, marital and sexual relations, inter-ethnic cooperation, contemporary political problems, women, Black American, Native America, and Third World issues, and the like are welcomed. Manuscripts must be equal to a 200 to 425 page book and are to be submitted in duplicate.

For additional information about this series or for the submission of manuscripts, please contact:

>Peter Lang Publishing, Inc.
>Acquisitions Department
>275 Seventh Avenue, 28th floor
>New York, New York 10001

To order other books in this series, please contact our Customer Service Department:

>800-770-LANG (within the U.S.)
>(212) 647-7706 (outside the U.S.)
>(212) 647-7707 FAX

Or browse online by series at:

>www.peterlang.com